Peter Livingston

## Poems and Songs

With lectures on the genius and works of Burns, and the Rev. George

Gilfillan; and letters on Dr. Dick, the Christian philosopher, and Sir J.

Franklin & the Arctic regions. Tenth Edition

Peter Livingston

**Poems and Songs**
*With lectures on the genius and works of Burns, and the Rev. George Gilfillan; and letters on Dr. Dick, the Christian philosopher, and Sir J. Franklin & the Arctic regions. Tenth Edition*

ISBN/EAN: 9783337328887

Printed in Europe, USA, Canada, Australia, Japan

Cover: Foto ©Thomas Meinert / pixelio.de

More available books at **www.hansebooks.com**

# POEMS AND SONGS;

WITH

## Lectures on the

# GENIUS & WORKS OF BURNS,

AND THE

## REV. GEO. GILFILLAN,

AND

## LETTER ON SIR JOHN FRANKLIN,

### AND THE ARCTIC REGIONS.

## BY PETER LIVINGSTON,

DUNDEE

—" A wish—I mind its power,
A wish that to my latest hour,
   Shall strongly heave my breast;
That I, for poor auld Scotland's sake,
Some useful plan or book could make,
   Or sing a sang at least."

———

TENTH EDITION,

———

DUNDEE:
PRINTED BY J. PELLOW, 10 TOP OF MURRAYGATE.

———

1858.

# CONTENTS.

# GEO. DUNCAN, ESQ., M.P. FOR DUNDEE.

DUNDEE, *26th January* 1852.

HONOURED SIR,

In dedicating to you the Eighth Edition
of the Poems and Songs of my Son, Peter Livingston,
and also his. Lecture on the Genius and Works of
Burns, as well as his Oration on the Rev. George Gil-
fillan, his genius and his criticism, I mentioned to you
that one of my reasons for the publication was, in con-
sequence of having to relinquish an extensive business
in the book trade, occasioned by severe personal afflic-
tion, during a period of more than ten years; and also
to do justice to my own feelings, as well as to fulfil a
wish of the Author; your honour having formerly be-
come his first subscriber for the original edition, the
sale of which was considerable;—the Seven Editions
extending to upwards of 6000 copies.

These are some of the reasons which have induced
me to solicit your indulgence; and I shall never forget
the kind and generous manner in which you not only
permitted the dedication, but feelingly expressed, that
if your consent could be of any service in forwarding
my design, it would afford you the utmost pleasure.

Allow me, dear Sir, simply to say, that I sincerely thank you for this expression of your kindness. And I beg leave to add, that so long as Dundee is screened from the northern blast by the beautiful hill behind it —so long as the grass grows on the Magdalen Green— so long as the border of that green is adorned by the *Vine*—so long as your school shall exist for the instruction of ₁poor children—so long will the name of George Duncan be held in grateful remembrance— and that you may live long to enjoy that popularity and esteem which you have so honourably earned, is

HONOURED SIR,

The earnest wish of your faithful and obedient Servant,

WILLIAM LIVINGSTON.

---

* The Beautiful Villa of the Honourable Member for Dundee.

# NOTICE OF THE AUTHOR.

THE Author of the following poems, songs, lectures, and letters, was born in Dundee, on the 20th of January 1823. His father, after residing twenty years in Perth, had removed at the previous Martinmas, and was for many years a bookseller and stationer in Dundee. His grandfather was James Livingston,—who, at the end of the last and the beginning of the present century, possessed a farm on the Laigh Fields of Hayston, in the parish of Glammiss, on the princely estate of the noble family of Strathmore—who expired three hours after the death of his second wife in 1826, and both were buried in one grave in Glammiss church-yard. His maternal grandfather was Charles Laing, a wright in Perth—was eminent for Christian piety. He died 1805; —the poet's mother is his oldest daughter.*

* Mr (afterwards Sir Walter) Scott, when about to publish one of his earliest works, was anxious to obtain some information about the classic ground of Lyndoch,—its mansion house, the grave of Bessy Bell and Mary Gray, all of which are so romantically situated on the banks of the Almond—and for that purpose waited on the amiable and aged Major Barry, then residing at Perth, but formerly proprietor and (with his equally amiable lady) improver of that beautiful estate. Having obtained from the Major ample information—particularly about the means he used to ascertain the exact spot where the bones of the beauties lay —the Major's servant (afterwards the poet's mother) was desired

During his infancy and childhood he exhibited an affectionate and kindly disposition, and a contemplative turn of mind maifested itself as his years' increased· When a mere boy, he greatly admired the preaching of the Rev. Mr Roxburgh of the Cross Church, and always spoke of him with the greatest enthusiasm. By a spark kindled at this flame, or some other cause, he about this time expressed an earnest desire to become a preacher; and in proof thereof, early in the mornings, would rise from his bed, place himself with a table and a Bible before him, inducing a younger brother to rise and sit in front of the table to act as precentor. Service was begun in right earnest; but sometimes the singing and often the sermon, would be interrupted by the visit of a pillow coming in contact, with the person of the orator, and make him bow to his audience, to the no small astonishment of the baby precentor,—this addition to the congregation being ejected from the bed of an elder brother, the preacher having disturbed the carpenter's repose.

Afterwards, the far-famed sermon, by the Rev. George Gilfillan, entitled "Hades, or the Unseen," made its appearance, and the poet took fire at what he considered severe criticism upon that production, and published a pamphlet in reply, entitled "Hades,

to place some refreshments on the table, when Mr Scott made some remarks on her beautifully fair hair; and he afterwards mentioned to one in the establishment of his publishers, that that, and her otherwise prepossessing and unassuming appearance sugges.ed to him the title of his novel, 'The fair Maid of Perth,'—and added, tradition has it, that Cathrine Glover, though well favoured and of ruddy countenance, was not fair but possessed of coal black hair.

or what has it's Opponents Proved?" in which, young
as he was, he defended some of the sentiments con-
tained in the sermon, and oppossed the ideas expressed
by the critics, with considerable ability, ingenuity, and
skill. Ere this some of his earliest verses appeared
in a few of the periodicals with which the locality was
then teeming; and they were generally well received,
which no doubt, induced him to collect and publish
them in a small volume, consisting of eight hundred
copies, which were all subscribed for in a very short
time. Thus encouraged, he composed some additional
pieces, which appeared in subsequent editions,—and in
visiting the neighbouring towns he was well patronised
and the press reviewed the work very favourably. At
Brechin, Lord Panmure patronised it very handsomely;
on going farther north, several hundred copies were sold
—and the Earls of Airlie and Kintore became sub-
scribers. Afterwards, his progress in Perth and Fife
was very successful, and the Professors of St Andrews
College nearly all subscribed; on visiting Edinburgh,
Lords Jeffrey and Robertson, with several of the other
Lords of Session, and a number of the Professors were
among his patrons; on going to Glasgow, two editions
of the work were called for, and the Earl of Eglinton
became its efficient patron. It may be here remarked,
that during the author's progress, as above stated, the
ministers of the Gospel of all denominations subscribed
for the work in great numbers, and their kindly senti-
ments often expressed towards him appeared to have left
a deep feeling of gratitude on his mind. He now went
to a celebrated college in England, where he studied
with success; afterwards preached with acceptance: de-

livered many orations, on theology and other popular subjects, among which was his lecture on Burns, and his feeling lecture on Dr Dick, the Christian Philosopher. He is now in London, on the wide field of literature. His oration on the Rev. George Gilfillan his genius and criticism, likewise his Letter on Sir John Franklin and the Arctic Regions, with lectures and addresses to various literary societies in and about the Metropolis, form part of his present efforts.

# ADDRESSED TO THE AUTHOR,

## By the late Lord Jeffrey.

～～～～～～

"24 MORAY PLACE, 30th December, 1846.

"DEAR SIR,

"I have now read through your little volume, and with very considerable satisfaction; but have scarcely anything to add to what I said to you personally, after I had perused but a part of it. The marked superiority of what I understand to be your later compositions gives good reason to look for still greater improvement in those you may produce in future; you are still young enough to contemplate great advances, and become a pleasing versifier, and express amiable sentiments and domestic affections in a natural and touching way.

"The thoughtful and tender parts are decidedly the best, and some of the songs are not without merit.

"You asked my SINCERE opinion of your work. The expression of it is, the talent you possess, if rightly estimated, may always afford you an innocent and elegant amusement, and obtain for you the notice and regard of many who may be of use to you: and with these advantages I trust you will have sense enough to be satisfied.

" In the meantime, believe me, with all good wishes,

Your faithful and obedient servant,

"F. JEFFREY."

" *To Mr Peter Livingston, Dundee.*"

The above letter was highly appreciated by the author, as a valuable gift from that prince of critics and highly-gifted and great man.

# SECOND EDITION

OF

## A LETTER,

### ADDRESSED TO THE QUEEN,

ON

# SIR JOHN FRANKLIN,

### AND THE

## ARCTIC REGIONS.

———◆———

MAY IT PLEASE YOUR MAJESTY,

The theme upon which I take the liberty
to address you is invested with a deep and distressing
interest.   There are concerned in it the lives and deaths
of many individuals, the hopes and fears of many hearts.
Your Majesty will pardon me being somewhat minute
—I shall not be lengthy—as, on this subject, I address
not your Majesty alone, but also the public, in whom
there exists an ardent desire to know all that can be
known on this important question.   It may be of im-
portance briefly to inquire into the causes that have led
to our earnest exertions on the subject.   Wherefore is
it that man has sacrificed life—left friends, home, and
country?   Why has Government spent so much money
and been so unwearied in its exertions to explore the

A

unknown regions of the North, where is nothing but eternal ice and snow? This question is answered to a certain extent by our knowledge of man's nature;—it is man's nature to enquire, to know, and to understand all that is round and about him. Man has got the earth for an inheritance, and he wishes to understand it. We do not like to live in a house without knowing its apartments. Such is the cause, found in man's nature, of all his intrepidity and daring. It is this that has led man forth with brave heart, to encounter all the dangers and difficulties which he is sure to meet with in his journyes over flood and field. It was this that led forth the great Columbus to find out the new world of the west, and has made him immortal for his enterprise and daring. This led forth the fearless Cook over the wide waste of waters which covered our earth like a shroud, in the midst of which he lighted on the Owhyee, where he fell a victim to the fury of the natives of a country into which he went intending to bequeath the blessings of civilization. This led Bruce to the mysterious Nile, and Park to the undiscovered Niger, where he too fell in the midst of those desert regions which have well been called the white man's grave. It is this desire to know that has made man to ascend the everlasting hills, penetrate the unknown deserts, and plant his foot on spots of the earth where the foot of man had never been before. And this desire it is, coupled with a love of gold (perhaps a commendable love of gold) which has led forth our daring mariners to explore those unknown regions of the North, where is nothing but everlasting ice and snow holding sway in the dismal wilderness.

It was doubtless a love of gold, in conjunction with

our thirst for knowledge, that has led to all our exertions to discover a North-west passage. The British Isles are situated on the globe so as to be far from many commercial ports of great importance in the world. On the west, we have the continents of North and South America between ourselves and the western shores of these continents. On the east, we have the continents of Europe and Africa between us and China and Hindostan. These facts were seen and known by our commercial men, and their desire to find a speedy passage to the western shores of America and the golden land of the east, found a ready response in the minds of our navigators, in whom there existed a desire to know if there was a way in the north by which they could sail round the world. The propriety, however, of any exertions on our part, and indeed at any time, may with some show of reason be questioned. In a commercial point of view, the passage, although discovered, could never be rendered available for any practical or useful purpose. In these regions the ice closes in upon us and thus seems to present a lasting barrier to man's progress in that direction.

Thus, although the passage were at once discovered those who come after the original explorers must have the same difficulties to encounter, the same natural impediments in their way that the original explorers had to contend with. Till the sun himself shall melt the everlasting hills of snow, man may never be permitted to approach these regions. Be this as it may, the necessity for further exertions on our part to discover a North-West Passage is now done away with; from the fact, that the railway by the Isthmus of Panama and the canal by Lake Nicaragua, as also the proposed railway accross the continent of Europe and direct from England to Indi a, will give us the desired end without having to encounter any of those physical difficulties which impede our progress in the Northern Seas.<sup>＊</sup>

This, however, is incidental; we have to deal with

＊ The two passages to which I have referred, will entirely do away with the necessity, in a commercial point of view, for our prosecuting the‘ discovery of a North-west Passage further. Those by the Isthmus of Panama and Lake Nicaragua will open up a floodgate of commercial prosperity to the world, which w have never known before : they will bring within a short dis tance of our shores the western coasts of North and South America ; they will also open up a direct passage to the vast Pacific Ocean, and to the many Islands which stud that Ocean, which are too numerous for me to name or to number. The Railway across the Continent of Europe from England to India is one of the most gigantic ideas ever conceived by the mind of man. When this Railway is completed,—which in the course of time, it doubtless will be,—the golden land of the East will be brought within a distance of seven days' journey from England. Thus do we stand in the prospect of seeing realized a fact so great and so gigantic that had it been told to our forefathers they must have deemed it little less than an Arabian tale. Many parties tell us that such a project can never be carried out ; doubtless to the minds of many, it may seem an impossi bility, but there is more in heaven and in earth than is dreamt of in their philosophy. In the vocabulary of some men there is no such word as fail ; and such men necessity will find to carry out this great undertaking. Not only will a Railway be laid down from England to the East, but we may not err in prognosticating that an Electric Telegraph will soon be laid down also. Then the pilgrim by the banks of the river Indus, and the hero of Hindostan may converse with his friends in fatherland : then will the daring fancy of our immortal Shakspeare be reduced to a vulgar reality, that of putting a girdle round the earth in forty minutes.

what has been done: the conclusions to which I have referred being come to, expeditions have from time to time been fitted out, only a passing allusion to several of which I can give before coming to that of Sir John Franklin; the voyages of Mackenzie, Davy, Beechy, the Rosses, Back, Dease, Simpson, and others, may be named as connected with our present subject. Captain Parry discovered many lands, bays, and large islands, the principal of which he named. Captain Ross discovered the large island of Boothia, which is thinly inhabited with Esquimaux These various expeditions and their sucesses, led to the expedition under the command of Sir John Franklin. That expedition left this country in the month of May, 1845; there were composing it in all, two ships, the Erebus and Terror, and 138 men; they took with them provisions calculated with economy to last four years and a half. Sir John Franklin's instructions were to proceed up by Davis' Straits to Baffin's Bay, so on to Lancaster Sound, Barrow Straits, and thus by Cape Walker, then to use his own discretion. The expedition was last seen in Baffin's Bay, bound to an iceberg waiting for a passage through the ice. Traces of Sir John Franklin's expedition have, however, since been found on Beechy Island, which is situated at the entrance to Wellington Channel. Here were found three graves of men who had been buried,—there where the white sea foam shall wash them daily; here also were found a carpenter's shop, a forge, a post, and several other sad memorials of the missing men.

This fact has led many to conclude—we think justly, —that Franklin must have penetrated in by Welling-

ton Channel and Victoria Channel, which is a continuation
of the former, and so on to the North Pole of the earth.
It seems very reasonable to come to this conclusion
from the fact, that it was Franklin's own impression
that the most likely way to discover a North-west Pas-
sage, if defeated in his course by Cape Walker, was to
proceed up Wellington Channel, and so on through
the Arctic Ocean, if possible, to Behring Straits.

Such are the simple facts connected with Franklin's
expedition into the Polar Sea, and the conclusions to
which we come regarding these facts lead us to believe,
that he may yet be found in these regions, and may yet
return from them.

We find that it is now upwards of six years since he
left this country, and he took with him provisions cal-
culated, with economy, to last four years and a half.
The question then presents itself to the mind, how can
Franklin and his companions have existed during the
year and a half beyond which his provisions were calcul-
ated to last. This question is answered to a certain
extent by our knowledge of the fact, that in these regions
he may have been able to procure rein-deer, white foxes,
seals, birds, and indeed various other animals which
abound in these northern regions. This supposition is
strongly confirmed, if it be not reduced to a certainty, by
our knowledge, that in the regions to which we suppose
Sir John Franklin must have gone, namely, Wellington
Channel and Victoria Channel, have been seen many speci-
mens of animal life, all of which could support Sir John
Franklin and his brave companions. That which makes
us urge this view of the question with the more earnest-
ness is, if Sir John Franklin has penetrated through Vic-

toria Channel, it is possible that he may now be in the Polar Sea, where he knew full well it is not so cold, and where animal life is much more plentiful than it is at what is cal'ed the magnetic pole of the earth. That Franklin did penetrate into Wellington Channel and Victoria Channel, we think there can now be no reasonable doubt.

We have before remarked, that it was Sir John Franklin's intention to proceed by Wellington Channel if defeated on his way by Cape Walker. This coupled with the fact that remains of the expedition have been found on and beyond to the north of Beechy Island seems to leave no reasonable doubt on the mind that he must have penetrated up that channel. Upon Beechy Island were found several sad and melancholy remains of the missing men. Here Franklin wintered in 1845-46; here also were found three graves—sublime in their loneliness—of men belonging to the expedition who had died. Here also were discovered a garden, a carpenter's shop, a forge, a post, and several other sad remains of the Northern voyagers Beechy Island is situated a little to the north of Cape Hotham, and therefore seems to be a favourable starting point for Wellington Channel and the Polar Sea. These facts, then coupled with Franklin's wish before he left this country to proceed in that direction, seem to warrant us in coming to the conclusion that he did penetrate into the Polar Sea, and having done so, we have more than one reason for believing that he may be there still.

The objections brought against this conclusion do not seem to carry with them much weight. Your Majesty is aware that there has been going the round of

the press a story to the effect that Sir John Franklin
and his companions have long since been murdered by a
hostile tribe of 'Esquimaux. This melancholy tale is
given to the world upon the authority of the veritable
Adam Beck, an Esquimaux, who, by virtue of the fact
that he can read and write well, was at once initiated
into the solemnity of an oath, and all the paraphernalia
of English justice. This absurd report has been charac-
terised by an able writer on the subject as a crude and
heartless tale. We can scarce doubt the propriety of
this conclusion. If such a report be true, did no one
see the murder but Adam Beck? If so, who were they
that saw it—are they living, or are they dead? Where
did it take place, and when did it take place? Did Sir
John Franklin leave no vestige behind? By whom was
he killed, and where was he buried? Let those questions,
and questions like them, be answered, till we see if this
tale be true. But I shall no longer weary the patience
of your Majesty with further allusion to this idle story;
I look upon it as a mockery and an insult to the judg-
ment of the British people. We are also told that his
ammunition may not have lasted; that the intense and
biting cold of these northern regions, so long continued
may ere this time have destroyed him, or that he may
have sunk a total wreck within the raging sea. All
these conclusions to this whole matter are doubtless pos-
sible, and cause conflicting feelings to cross the mind
when we contemplate the fate of the brave mainers.
Speculation regarding them seems, to a certain extent
out on a shoreless sea. But so long as there remains
the bare possibility of their existence, to that possi-
bility it is right for us to cling in hope, even though

that hope be so long deferred that it make the heart sick. This conclusion come to, then our duty in the matter seems palpable and plain. That duty seems to me to be to send out another expedition in search of the missing men. Let that expedition be well fitted out; let it also be done speedily, so that in the spring-time of the year it may reach the Northern Seas. We have several reasons for coming to the conclusion that it is our duty to send out further expeditions in search of the missing men, in the first place, Sir John Franklin and his brave associates left their country, their friends, and their homes, in the service of the Government of the country to which they belong; Sir John Franklin and his companions have been tried and trusty servants of the state; they had done the State some service, and we know it; such being the case we conceive them to be fit and becoming objects of the State's care and protection. As a matter of justice alone it is our duty to do what we can for the safety of the missing men. This is our duty, on the ground of justice alone, what shall we say when we come to those of charity and mercy? Shall we stand idly looking on; shall we live at home, at ease; shall we sit under our own vine and fig-tree while our brethren, brave in heart and strong in arm, may still be living in the dark and dismal regions of the North, bound by eternal ice and snow?

Your Majesty, let it not be said that England can be guilty of this crime; let not the sin of ingratitude be laid to our charge. I have before given proofs of the means by which it is possible our countrymen may still be in existence. I spoke of the provision, of the means of living they might get in the North, reindeer, foxes, seals, birds, or indeed many other animals. I also referred to the fact, that the climate towards the pole of the earth is more congenial than it is towards the magnetic pole. All these things, I repeat, taken into consideration, give us proof that hope should not yet be dead within us; so long as there exists a single chance of their safety, we are bound to try to save them; thus our duty seems palpable and plain. We may rest upon our oars perhaps in sadness and in sorrow, till the dark days of winter have passed away, then when the spring time shall have come upon us, when the sun shall gild again the hills of everlasting snow, then let us heart and hand send out farther help and aid to our countrymen, so that, if still in existence, they may be saved from a watery grave.

It is true that our efforts may not be crowned with success, we may search for, and seek for, that which we cannot find; so let it be, if Providence will have it so; we cannot change it, but our duty done, we have gained for ourselves that self-satisfaction and peace which passeth all understanding. If our daring mariners are in the deep, we can only say it was the will of God, and may not be grieved at or mourned over.

If they are dead, they have fallen blessed martrys; after life's fitful fever they sleep well, with the sea for an everlasting mourer. But for the sake of the living, if not for the dead, by the blighted hopes and bleeding hearts of the mourning survivors; by the widow's tears, the orphan's cries, and the mother's crucified affections; by the honour of that great nation of which you are the head, do I call upon your Majesty, respectfully but earnestly, to use your royal prerogative and send out another expedition in search of the Northern explorers, so that our minds may be set at rest and kept no longer

on the rack, but that we may know the best or the worst
of this perplexing business. As we would, in conclu-
sion, humbly suggest to your Majesty the propriety that,
f it is to be done, it were well that it were done
quickly; there is now no time to be lost, for every day
may bring with it death. So long as a lingering hope
remains behind,—so long as there is a shadow of be-
lief that our countrymen may still be in life,—it is our
duty to try to save them.* Our duty done, we may
safely leave the rest with that providence who, in His
mercy, ever tempers the wind to the shorn lamb.

I have the honour to be,

Your Majesty's

Most obedient humble servant,

FETER LIVINGSTON.

---

* Farther traces of the missing expedition have been found ;
ships are being again sent out by the Goverment, under the
command of Sir Edward Belcher, and Dr. Rae overland, in search
of Sir John Franklin and his companions.

# LECTURE ON ROBERT BURNS.

ROBERT BURNS—Scotland's best and greatest poet—was born on the 25th of January 1759, in a small cottage about two miles from the town of Ayr. He was ushered into this world amid storm and darkness. Part of the house in which he was born, just as he saw the light, was blown in by the tempest; the new-made mother, with her baby boy, sought and received shelter from a neigh-bour. His father, William Burns, had been a farmer; but worldly adversity compelled him to betake himself to the field as a labourer. Robert at the age of six was sent to school, where, under Mr John Murdoch, a man of whom the poet makes honourable mention, he remained two years. Here he acquired reading, grammar, and some knowledge of the French language. Beyond this he had not much of what is called school education, but as we shall hereafter see, he was " quick to learn and wise to know."

He was at an early age somewhat fortunate in the books he read, having a few of Shakspeare's Plays, Locke on the Understanding, Ramsay's Poems, along with other books of value.

It was between the fifteenth and seventeenth years of his age that Burns first wrote poetry. Love was the mother of his muse. He was early blest with what was early blighted—his love for Highland Mary. This was a sacred affection, almost too pure for earth. She died; alas! too early—died as all the good die— loving, hoping

Burns, when a young man, engaged in partnership with a flaxdresser; but, in a happless hour, the premises took fire and left the poet pennyless. He now took the farm of Mosgeil, in conjunction with his brother Gil bert, a man of sound understanding. Here Burns first met Jean Armour, afterwards his wife; and their firs intimacy ended in misfortune. Our poet now looked to a foreign land for that peace and prosperity which his own denied him. He resolved to go to Jamaica and published his poems to provide him with the neces-saries for the voyage. These wild irregular utterings came upon the world to make it wonder and admire. He was at once exalted from the condition of a plough-man to that of the first poet of his country. *He changed his plans; was advised to go to Edinburgh. He did so, as we shall hereafter see, to his sorrow. He became a lion among the literary men of the great city. The Ayrshire ploughman sat at the tables of the nobility—drank wine,—they taught him to drink deep ere he de-parted,—he here carried a Duchess off her feet with the brilliancy of his conversation—fell in love with the charm-ing Clarinda,—and indulged too often in wild potations. This could not last long; he sought peace and something permanent. He left the gay city; took the farm of Ellisland; spent too much time in preparing for his wife; and the habits he had contracted in Edinburgh sometimes' assailed him. He was now appointed to the Excise. A ludicrous mistake. Burns was seen sounding the depth of whisky casks when he should have been hold-ing the plough. This man's days and pleasures on earth were brief, but not delightful. The earthly tabernacle gave way under the fiery spirit. His body was racked with pain; there was malady in his soul. He tried all

B

things; all would not do. Death was upon him. The strong man was bowed down—the daughters of music were brought low—desire had failed, and all was darkness. In the thirty-eight year of his age this great man, after severe bodily and mental suffering, yielded up his spirit into the hands of Him who gave it.

Such is a brief account of the career of Robert Burns. Gentlemen, this man's life was a tragedy in one act Like all other great tradgedies there was much glory, much sublimity, much beauty, and much truth in it. There were besides, interspersed throughout, a few comic scenes, and good. Burns, when a young man, was a happy man; and, during the whole of his life, he had seasons of exalted, yea, delirious joy. This we are glad to know and say; but taking it all and all, it were difficult to point out a story of more woe than that of Robert Burns.

Born amid poverty, this were nothing,—bred to the plough, would be had never left it,—touched by the empyrean fire of genius, honourable ambition seized his soul; it was first fed, then foully abused; he was exalted to a giddy height of glory, placed at length upon a pinnacle of fame, from which he did not fall but which fell under him; and when he did come down, he fell, like Lucifer, but, so far as this world is concerned, never to rise again.

Gentlemen, I do not mourn over the life of Burns as many do. I do not mourn over it for the world's sake: but I mourn over it for his own. Even then we need not become very pathetic. What was the the world to him? He seems to have been born not so much to live as to fly across life " like a fierce comet of tremendous
ɛ, bidding the nations to wonder as he passed."

Many point to him, and say " You see what he was, what might he have been ?" We venture into no such dangerous speculations. We are thankful for him as he was; and as for the world, why he was more to the world than the world was to him. .

It is my impression that the most unfortunate, not to say the most fatal, step in the life of Burns, was his visit to Edinburgh.

I know that, at the time, this step was necessary; we, nevertheless, regret the effects that flowed from it. Burns went among the great folk there as a world's wonder. They kept him such during his stay. He left them and was forgotten by them. It was a natural result. He said, he knew it should be so. He said he would bear it like a man. Doubtless he thought he would and could do so. It turned out to be easier to say this than to do it. He was forgotten, but could not in his turn forget. When the trumpet of fame ceased to sound at his coming, the remembrance of what he once was rose up before him, to heat his very brains, to crucify his soul, and to send him, or do much to send him to an untimely grave. Edinburgh did more ill to Burns than all this. It did not rob him of his independence—this was past the power of man; but it robbed him to a great extent of his self-dependence, which was a gigantic evil. He was a great poet, and as such, could not brook the idea of again becoming a ploughman. I blame no one for this; I pity all concerned, and speak for the future. In this matter the world has yet to learn a lesson. We must not neglect genius, but we must not abuse it; we must not kill it with kindness. We must not deprive it of purpose and

aim in life. We must teach it that it has to work and
live in this world as well as to tell the world truths.
Burns was treated in much the same way as a few well.
meaning men lately treated William Thom. They took
him to London; gave him dinners; drove him about in
carriges; took him through the great city to see and be
seen. He left them at last, and died a beggar—broken-
hearted.

Far better would we treat genius were we to put a
spade in its hand, and say " Go now and till the soil,
bring forth good fruit,—feel great truths and tell them,
—be a blessing to thyself and mankind; show to the
world that you are a God-sent man."

Thus do we leave the life of Burns; we come now to
his character. The tongue of slander, slaked over as it
is by the venom of vile thought, has been busy with this
man's memory. Far be it from me to say he was in-
fallible. We are not blind to his errors. We think he
sinned not a little, and suffered much. But we are
strong in the belief that we shall be able to repel many
of the charges that have been brought against him. We
humbly think that we shall be able to prove that since
his death he has been more sinned against than he ever
sinned, by men to whom (as it has been well said) he
was as superior in virtue as he was in genius.

First of all, he has been called an uneducated man.
Secondly he has been called an irreligious man. Thirdly
he has been called an immoral man.

I shall notice these charges in the order in which
they are here set down. First of all, he has been called
an uneducated man. This charge is true only to a certain
extent. He had not what is called a classical education.
He did not know Hebrew; he did not know Greek.

He did not read so many books as we in this age of
wondrous wisdom are supposed to read; but therein he
was wise, and it was well. If he did not read so much
as we do, he perhaps thought more. He was not an
educated man in the high sense of the term, but he
cannot with truth be called an unlearned man. He read
his Bible, he read Milton, he read Shakspeare; and who
will tell me that the man who reads and understands
these books as Burns did, can remain uneducated? But
above and beyond all this, Burns was learned, deeply
learned, in the mysteries of the human soul; he was a
philosopher by inspiration. But further still, Burns
was taught, and taught profoundly, too, by the book of
nature, which was his favourite book. He gazed upon
the stars, which were to him then what they are to us now,
the poetry of heaven; the wind, when it blew high, rock-
ing castles, telling the wretch to tremble, and letting the
world know that the Lord was abroad, was to him a source
of deep inspiration. The trees, bending beneath the blast
as if in adoration of their God, taught him a lesson of
devotion. The morning star, as it l ingered between day-
light and darkness, wafted his soul to heaven as it died
away. He saw the moonbeam sleeping in the waters,
and he said it was no purer than the love of a true wo·
man's soul. A summer cloud, floating in the blue hea-
ven, like the last vestige of the breath of God, could not
pass over him without his special wonder. Spring with
her beauty—Autumn with her ¦bounty—Summer with
her golden sunshine—and Winter, with her sheet of snow
—to him were teachers all The flowers of earth were
dear to him; the rosebud blushing in the morning dew
—the lily, pale as the cheek of a dying child—the daisy,
modest as the blush of a young maiden—he loved them

all. The birds, too, earth's sweetest choristers, were his delight. The lark's loud song at heaven's gate—the cuckoo, welcome with the spring—the robin's sweet domestic chirp—the lapwing, lamenting the loss of her love,—all, all were very dear to him Nature, in all her phases, was to him an exceeding joy. The solitary cottage on the desert moor, with its reek curling to the clouds—the lonely cairn on the mountain side, touched his soul with reverence for the glory of the past. The shepherd in his grey plaid, under the old oak tree—the milkmaid's song, the loud laugh of playful children—cattle grazing in the field—sheep at the fell—all were very dear to him. His book, we say, was the book of nature, and by it he was taught profoundly. We but show our want of education when we say Burns was an uneducated man

It has also been said that Burns was an irreligious man. I do not believe it, but I deny it. This slander was first sent abroad by those among whom Burns mingled, and it was sent abroad because he differed in opinion from them. Burns did differ in religious opinion from the times in which he lived, and the men among whom he mingled; but to call him irreligious because he did this, is to take him up before he has fallen. For a man to differ from the religion of his time is, I maintain, no proof that that man is irreligious. After this fashion, Socrates was irreligious. According to the fashion which they call heresy, Paul worshipped the God of his fathers. Because Burns after this fashion differed from his fellow-men, he has been called irreligious. We stay not here to enquire what was the religious belief of the times in which Burns lived; our business now simply is, to prove that Burns was no irreligious man. To that do we now address ourselves. Let us first of all take a broad view of the man. Burns believed in God. He believed in Christ, and loved and admired the beauty of his character. He believed in immortality, and while here, longed much for another and a better world. If these statements be true, we think it would be hard to prove that the man who held such opinions was irreligious. But above and beyond all this, we believe that Burns was not a irreligious man, because of the general tenor of his writings. As proof of this, witness his many letters, in which he speaks of religion. Witness also his many poems wherein he refers to the subject. His "Cottar's Saturday Night," a strain which, without profanity be it spoken, angels might admire. I would direct attention to several, written to Mrs Dunlop, and one to his friend Cunningham. His " address to Mary in heaven," wherein he "holds communion with the sainted spirit of his first affection, each word sealed with a tear and a sigh, the purest that ever flowed on earth, and the sincerest that was ever uplifted to heaven." Above all, remember his own declaration that an irreligious poet was a monster. This we conceive to be perfectly true. But we go beyond it, and we say that an irreligious poet were not only a monster, but an irreligious poet is an impossibility. There can be no such thing. No such being ever walked God's earth. Shelley said there was no God, but he did not believe it. Byron, for all his waywardness, said, what we believe to be true, that he was readier to die than the world supposed him to be. So was it with Burns. We look in vain in the world for an irreligious poet. What is a poet ? He is the very man above all others who cannot be irreligious.

He is a being who feels great truths, and tells them;
whose soul is attuned to the harmonies of nature. He
cannot, even if he would, turn against the giver of his
gift; he must be true to his mission, true to God.
Such was Burns. Both in word and deed scorning and
giving the lie to much of the world's morality, and also
its religion; he was, nevertheless, not an irreligious man.
His soul was deeply imbued with the spirit of nature,
open to the breath of God. He reverenced all that was
divine and holy, and admired, with a devout admiration,
beauty and truth.

Burns has been called an immoral man. In answer-
ing this charge we must take a broad view of the man,
and a liberal view of human nature. Man is a com-
bination, shall I not say, of good and evil. He has a
body, which is of the earth, earthy; a soul, which is of
heaven, heavenly: he is a compound of sense and soul
—the quintessence of dust and deity; he has two na-
tures, what the Scriptures expressively call the carnal
and the spiritual—the one leads to what we call good,
the other to what we call evil. To take this view of
human nature is, I think, the best, perhaps the only
way in which we can account for the actions of our
great men; while, at the same time, it leads us to have
but little sympathy with that erring philosophy which
has been propounded by the living, sitting in stupid
wonder, over the sepulchres of the dead, bespattering
the departed spirits of the mighty great with condem-
nation—making them out to be demons only. Equally
vain is that philosophy which, in opposition to this, has
made out our great men to be angels. The truth is
wholly with neither of these parties. Those among
men who have had the hoof of the fiend, have also had

the tongue of the angel. Giant sons of God, great in good and great in 'evil, but ever great; now grovelling in earth, now aspiring to heaven. Thus do we account or the lewdness of Voltaire, the vulgarity of Paine, the misanthropy of Byron, the atheism of Shelley, the debauchery of Burns, the ambition of Bonaparte.

Looking, then, at human nature in this light, we cannot and do not deny but Burns had strong passions; sometimes they laid him low, and stained his name. But because of this, for his fellowmen to bring against him the general charge of immorality, is to sin against the living and slander the dead. If Burns had the vices of mankind, he also had their virtues—if he sinned he suffered; and we hope that he was made pure through suffering. He was a dutiful son, a loving husband, an affectionate father—what more can mortal be. These general charges, damning to the memory of man, are brought against Burns, and such as he, by men who have neither his power to do good, nor his power to do evil; by men whose chief delight it is eternally to rake up the ashes of the dead, and rail on the Lord's anointed. Thus do we hurl back these strictures, and for ever consign them to the tomb of all the Capulets, that from it there may be no after resurrection.

We come now to the writings of Burns, before which however, we have one other charge to refer to, one other murmur to chastise and rebuke. He has been accused of writing no long poem. Now when will this (as it would seem everlasting) murmuring cease? Had the man not liberty to write what he pleased? Who has a right to accuse him for what he has not done? Burns was, like all the truly great, too great for writing books. The truly great among men write no books—they have too much faith for this; they do with their thoughts what we are told to do with our bread—cast them on the waters, believing that, after [many days, they will find them safe. Socrates wrote no books—he just uttered his thoughts, and, once uttered, they were ever immortal. So it is with our own Shakspeare; he, while living, wrote no books; he wrote a few irregular poems, which modern admiration and art hath collected into a book; but the thoughts expressed of such men live long after books have crumbled into the dust from whence they came.

So it was with Burns, he wrote no long book; he could not be forever inspired. The wind bloweth where it listeth—he wrote when the spirit moved him. He wrote no great epic; but his poems, when collected together, may be said to be one great and glorious lyric; abrupt, irregular, lofty, sublime, soft and tender. ravishing the soul. He was great " either for tragedy, comedy, history, pastoral, pastoral-comical, pastoral-historical, tragical-historical, tragical comical, historical pastoral; scene individual, or poem unlimited." Now moving you to tears, now convulsing you with laughter; now lifting you to heaven on the wings of the wind; anon chaining you with love's willing fetters as he mourns the loss of his Mary. Now singing a song to rouse up the patriotic love of a people against oppression. Now inditing his verses to the mouse, wherein he shows us that the humblest thing in God's creation is the earth-born companion and fellow-mortal of man.

In his " Cottar's Saturday Night" he has lit the lamp of love, and poured a gleam of glory round the family altar. In his " Man was made to Mourn," he has given us a gloomy view of man, and told us some truths which the world will not willingly let die. In his " Tam o'

Shanter" he draws a picture of pleasure, and sums up the whole in words not soon to be forgotten. In his "Epistle to a Young Friend," he has shown that he was both poet and philosopher. In his "Address to the De'il," he gives us proof of the charity that was in his soul, for he tells us that even he may have a stake in heaven. In his song of "a Man's a Man for a' that," he shows us that a true soul can beat under a tattered garment as well as beneath a Roman toga.

It was the mission of Burns to bind man to man—to teach us love and kindness—to soothe the sorrows—to sing the joys, to lighten the labour of the poor—to vindicate the dignity of the mind—to speak trumpet-tongued against oppression, and make us in love with liberty—to tell the world great truths, which the world must one day believe. All this has he done, and in doing this he made life more delightful by the rich feast of poetry and music which he hath provided for his fellow-men.

Burns was a remarkable writer in prose as well as poetry, though his poetry has eclipsed his prose Like Milton, he has hitherto been remembered chiefly as a poet. Still the letters of Burns are remarkable productions. I grant that in them we behold him too often on stilts. But all things considered, we cannot but wonder that in his letters there is so much that is noble, good, and true Had it been a peer, instead of a ploughman that wrote them, and had he, the peer, died young, men would have said that he was a wild and wonderful genius, and but wanted years to amaze mankind. I know few books of the same dimensions from which so many beauties could be culled as from the letters of Burns.

"The poetic genius of my country found me as the prophetic bard Elijah did •Elisha—at the plough, and threw her inspiring mantle over me." Such is the language of the poet. We do not wonder at the fact, we only name it. Heaven and earth are full of poetry; and nature, when she wished a voice wherewith to speak had as good right to choose her man from the plough as from the professor's desk. Fergusson the astronomer was a shepherd boy. Bloomfield the poet was a shoe maker. Burns was bred at the plough. God is with his children everywhere to bless them and to do them good.

Such was Burns, such is the legacy he has left to man. His place as a poet we do not and cannot fix; but he has well been called one of brightest stars shining round the sun—Shakspeare.

Thus let him be—thus let him shine. So long as the thistle bends to the blast—so long as the heather grows in the sun, and gilds the mountain top—so long as honest men and bonny lasses people the town of Ayr— so long as birds sing from the bush, and flowers are beautiful—so long as grass waves green on the banks o' bonny Doon—so long as man loves woman, and woman trusts to man—so long shall Burns be remembered. I bid farewell to his memory with gratitude and joy. I rejoice at the opportunity I now have had of strewing this frail garland of love and admiration on his glorious grave.

# GEORGE GILFILLAN,

## AND HIS WRITINGS

GEORGE GILFILLAN is a remarkable man. He is the
critic of the present age, as Byron was the poet thereof
some years ago. Gilfillan the critic, like Byron the
poet, has not had to climb up the hill of fame; but, from
the natural height on which he found himself exalted,
he has lighted down upon its top, whereon he now sits
enthroned in the garb of immortality. The critic, like
the poet, has by one giant stride, outstripped all his con_
temporaries. What it took them years of labour
to accomplish, he has by one great effort achieved.
Gilfillan as a critic, has the power and eloquence of
Macaulay; the sparkling brilliancy of Jeffery; the wild-
ness if not the wit of Sidney Smith; is just and unerring
in his judgments as Hazlitt. Above and beyond this, he
has an eloquence belonging to himself, peculiarly his own.
He has among other things written a book, called "a
Gallery of Literary Portraits," which has given him—
who six years ago was not known—a fame, which, if not
as yet European, is at least British and American.
Gilfillan is a painter, and has drawn the mental
characteristics of the most eminent literary men of the
present and past generations:

Jeffrey—alas! we can no longer say as Byron said,
health to him; but we can at least and do say, peace
to the memory of the great immortal—Christopher
North among the Mountains,—Chalmers, fit follower of

the Apostle Paul,—Emerson the transcendentalist deeply embued with the spirit of nature,—Wordsworth king of rocky Skiddaw, now no more (the stars are falling from us; the firmament is all but left in darkness! Even the harp of Erin is broken among the mountains, it is now for ever silent, and no longer vibrates to the passing breeze); Carlyle the thinker deep and strong; Byron a weed thrown on the water; Shelley the enthusiast; Coleridge the dreamer; and many more, are treated of in this delightful book

Gilfillan is not only a clever man, but he is a man of the highest talents, of the most exalted genius. This gift from God—genius—quivers in his tremulous lip, distends his keen nostril, and flashes in his fiery eye. His intellect is piercing; what other men see as through a glass darkly, is, to his keen vision, as the bright and broad noon day. He is guided by the light not of cleverness or talent only, but of genius; and thus gifted, he leaps, as if by instinct, to a conclusion regarding the mental qualities of an author, in a way which almost invariably insures success and certainty. In his analysis of an author, Gilfillan takes hold of him frankly and freely. He looks at him from top to toe, turns him round about and round about, lifts him up and down, and scrutinizes him in every possible way. He surveys him from all points, and is monarch of all he surveys. Thus the very shades of his author's meaning are caught every phase of his mind is laid hold of, and put down palpably upon the printed page. It is an eloquent and glowing book, full at once of love, benevolence, and stern truth. It awakens the finest feelings of the soul; while you read it your blood runs cold and warm at once. In a langnage which is now withered and now wild in its attire, the author does much to make us love, with a still fonder affection, the truly great—nature's nobles, those who have left behind them a legacy for the good of man. We are transported with the author, wander where he will—and where has he not wandered? He is a divine with Irving, a historian with Macaulay, an astronomer with Nichol, and a poet with Keats. When he reviews "Chalmer's Astronomical Sermons," you fancy yourself seated on a golden cloud, and feel in a fit humour for Festus to be by your side. In his notice of "Carlyle's French Revolution," he hurries you through that scene of blood, and makes you, for the time being, sup full of horrors. He has elevated many of his heroes to heaven, and is wonderfully eloquent when speaking of death. When he relates the sad fate of Shelley, who perished in the waters, the soul is moved with thoughts that are too deep for tears. In his article on Wordsworth, he beautifully shews that the mission of the true poet is high and holy, God-like and great. He, too, has exalted the lowly, lifted up the fallen; and one must ever regret, that Keats had not Gilfillan instead of Gifford for his reviewer. He has in a few instances dragged from obscurity men who, but for him, might long have blushed unseen. It may be unlike the law of nature, nevertheless so it is—the stars are made brilliant in the glory and light of the sun. Embalmed in his eloquence, they now bid fair for immortality; they shall now be known and remembered so long as truth and beauty are loved among men. With all his benevolence and kindness, which we so much admire, he is always truthful and stern, sometimes sarcastic and severe. One thing that will strike the reader of Gilfillan is his wonderful power of concentration, giving us much thought in few words. Thus we have a history of the literature of America in a few pages; and taking it as a whole, we cannot doubt its correctness. We have also an account of the various kinds of preaching graphically given in a page or two. We lately read to a learned German friend, a single passage from this book, that in reference to the leading German writers, in the review of Carlyle; our friend was astonished, and said that although he had read, ere now, volumes on the same authors, he had not before so succinct and clear an idea of their various merits. The book before us is calculated to cultivate the affections, to ele‑ vate the soul, to lift it from the grovelling things of earth to the better things of heaven. It does much to bind us in a bond of eternal union to the mighty living and the mighty dead; and more than all does it bind us in a love which language is poor to express—to God, from whom the gifted among men receive their power and greatness.

About Gilfillan's style we know not what to say. He is master of all kinds of style, and in his book are all kinds. The plain, the neat, the elegant, the florid, are familiar to him. He can turn a period with his pen as easy as a sugar plum in his mouth. He does not think much, if at all, of style; he is out of his "Blair's Rhetoric" long ago. As a general rule, however, there is about his style a reckless, revelry, a will savagery, pro‑ found, and deep and strong. There is, moreover, the glow of poetry ever hanging over it, which renders i mellow and beautiful, pleasing to the soul.

Gilfillan has faults, he is too great to be perfect. He quotes by far too many pretty bits from the poets, which, along with his own beauties, make his pages run over with sweets.

Besides the volume to which we have referred, our author has published several other things, all of them more or less characteristic. Sermons and lectures have at intervals come from his pen. He also writes among other things in " Hogg's Instructor," a series of papers called a " Bundle of Books." In one of these he lately smote our humble selves, in a way which though ticklish at the time, we now thank him for, and hope it improved us.*

*The late respected and favourite Provost Burnes of Montrose, when shewing the writer of this note several relics of his cousin the poet, pointed out the letter sent by Robert on the death of his father, in which were the words, "I have lost one of the best of fathers." On finishing the sentence, Burns' tears had evidently begun to flow, for their indentation was visible on the paper below the line ; the sight of which led to some conversation on the sensitiveness of authors. The Provost remarked, "I can give an instance of this in Robert's own case. When Will Nicoll and the poet were returning from their northern tour, my father and myself went out as far as Marykirk to meet them; among the first words Robert said, after kindly embracing us was, I have been at our paternal farm in the Mearns, and showed our old cousin some things I have wrote by the way, which I mean to publish,—but the farmer streekit himself up, gave a knap with his stick on the floor, and said, 'fie, fie, man, are you gaen to affront your respectable friends, by printing godless nonsense, na, na, gie me them and I'll put them in the fire.' The incident was then alluded to with evident chargin, before the poet left Montrose,—and his old cousin was no great favourite with Robert as long as he lived. [This note is inserted with the view to show the extreme sensibility of most authors.]

Mr Gilfillan has also just published a second "Ga'lery of Literary Portraits," a work somewhat like the first. To it we cannot in the meantime particularly refer. He says it is written in a tone more subdued than his former book. For some reasons we like this, for others we do not. Gilfillan should take care how he *subdues* himself. For ourselves, we are willing to tolerate a good deal of extravagance when we have his fire and truth. He will understand us, when we say that the lion wanting his mane is no longer king of the forest. The sun in a mist is no such glorious thing as when he goes through the heavens with his locks of golden fire.

Our author is also about to publish a work on the "Hebrew Bards." We do not, as a wretched critic lately said in the *Athenæum*— a journal which is day by day sinking in the estimation of all honest men—a journal which, unless it changes its course, will sink and sink speedily till it can sink no more,—a journal which of late has been as remarkable for its false philosophy as for its bad grammar; for a recent specimen of both of which, witness its review of the noble genius David Scott,—a journal notorious for its vile and heartless attacks on *the three men* of this present generation, —the trinity of talent,—Carlyle, Gilfillan, and Emerson; to whom no parallel, not the most distant comparison, can, in these days of ours, be found. We do not, like this journal, look forward to the appearance of Gilfillan's book with "awe and apprehension;" but we look forward to its coming with impatient expectation, hope, and joy. We fancy that here Gilfillan will rise to the height of his great argument, and soar away into regions which even he has never reached before. Indeed, Gilfillan has not got done nearly all that he can do.* The world has reason to expect great things from him in time to come. He has hitherto been, to a certain extent, by the high-ways and bye-ways of the world; a gatherer of weeds and wild flowers that grow rank upon the mountain side, many of which, wanting his fostering aid, would have wasted their sweetness in the desert air. We have hope that he will one day give us a full length portrait of Jesus. His picture of a prophet, in the notice of Shelley, shews his ability for the task. We know no pen of the present age more fit for the theme than Gilfillan's. We can fancy how great would be his picture of Christ—he who was God among men. Deep into time, and through the dim vista of far distant years, he had an eye to pierce; he sounded the depths of eternity; he lived in the future, and liveth now. The mantle of the everlasting fell upon him while he slept in the manger; and he rose from the river Jordan embalmed in the spirit of God.

We must now say a word respecting the personal history and personal appearance of our author. He was born at Comrie in Perthshire, where, we have heard him say that his cradle was rocked by the earthquake. There is poetry in everything he says. He studied at Glasgow University for the ministry. At college he was a great devourer of books; the fruits of which are now seen in his writings. He panted not for college honours; the greatest honour to him evidently being to get enshrined

*Since the above was written, " The Bards of the Bible " has appeared ; we hesitate not to pronounce it one of the most sublime creations of genius that was ever laid at the feet of him who bore the cross—the production and fruit of undying inspirations.

in the hearts of the people. He is now, and has been
for several years, pastor of a large and flourishing con-
gregation in Dundee, connected with the United Pres-
byterian Church. Here he labours, beloving and beloved.
Some persons who know nothing of him, and little of
anything else, have shaken their heads and shrugged their
shoulders, and wondered much if he could pay attention
to his clerical duties and write so many books. There is
more in heaven and earth than is dreamed of in their
philosophy. Do they imagine for a moment that they can
repress the out pourings of a soul bursting with the beau-
tiful in nature and in man? Gilfillan is only now spread-
ing abroad that which years of reading and reflection in
former days enabled him to store up in his mind. He is
thirty-nine years of age; tall, but not stout according
to the fashion of Old Joe in " Barnaby Rudge," he is,
however, what a connoisseur in these matters—which
we are not—would call a muscular man. His hair is
dark brown, inclining to curl; his brow, broad and high.
As if his far-seeing mind took him away from the power
of his natural vision, he wears spectacles. In his walk on
the street there is something very odd; and it has often
struck us that there is something remarkable in the walk
of many great men. That of Emerson is a calm and
holy soliloquy; that of Professor Wilson the unfinished
fragment of a great epic; that of Gilfillan a fiery ode.
You see at once that he is son of the mountains. In
the pulpit or on the platform there can be no mistake
about him. Whether sitting or standing he seems some-
what fidgetty, and you see at once that he is something
to look upon. In speaking, he is dreadfully in earnest.
Elocution as an art he has never studied; nevertheless

he is, as Dr Chalmers was, and as all earnest men must ever be, an elocutionist. When wishing to impress some great truth upon his hearers, there is a rude grandeur about his manner that is truly sublime. He holds you with his " glistening eye," 'and gives out his words in a voice now loud and long, as thunder among the mountains; anon deep and low, like the dying cadence of a powerful gong, sounded to summon the loitering idlers of a baron's hall to a Christmas feast. As he utters the last word he seems to get relieved of a burden that press ed hard upon him, and he rises like a giant renewed in his strength, fresh for another effort.

For the present our brief labour of love is ended. Farewell! thou great and gifted spirit,—thine is a soul prophetic burning with true fire. Thou hast made us more and still more in love with the beautiful in nature and the noble in man; and in doing this, thou art working at once for an earthly immortality, for an inheritance in heaven.

# LETTER ON DR DICK,

## THE CHRISTIAN PHILOSOPHER.

SIR*—Can we stand idly on, can man, can humanity stand idly on? Is the old tragedy once again to be enacted? Has blind Homer, the ballad-singer, taught us nothing? Do the voices of the dead call to us in vain? From the graves of Burns, Chatterton, and Thom, do we learn nothing? If so, then let the dead past bury the dead. How fares the living? Alas, there are at the present moment prophets being neglected amongst us. There is a popular authoress, a woman, and an ornament to womankind, she is in poverty; the Christian philosopher, Dr Dick is also overlooked. Can such things be and overcome us like a summer cloud, without our special wonder. Here is a man, over whose eloquent pages millions in this country, in Europe, and America, have hung with rapture and pondered with profit. Here is the man, who has done more than any other man we know, to popularise science among the people.

The man who has written the " Christian Philosopher," in which he speaks of the works of God; and shows that in wisdom he hath made them all,—the man who has written the philosophy of a future state in which he has built up our hope; confirmed our faith in another and better world,—the man who has written

---

* This Letter was written for the *Cardiff and Merthyr Guardian.*

the " Sidereal Heavens," in which he holds communion
with the Stars, and talks to the sun as to a play-fellow,
—the man who has done all this, and much more than
this; he who has given the world so much bread, has
received in return for his gift a stone.

The British Parliament, as we think, is in many re-
spects a good parliament. It is in many respects a good
political parliament. But in one thing we think it is
very deficient,—that is, in its patronage of good and
great men. All parliaments are, and ever have been,
deficient in this. We however offer this complaint
more in sorrow than in anger. Parliament cannot do
everything. We very often ought to be doing ourselves
when we are babbling about the duties of parliament.
Let it be so now; let us have home reformation. Let
us assist ourselves, and our fellowmen who have done
us good. With this feeling, I call upon Scotchmen; I
call upon Englishmen and Irishmen; I call upon Britain
not to let this man, of whom I have been speaking, die
neglected. He will die some day; in the course of na-
ture, that day cannot be far distant; and when he does
die, we shall all then make a universal rush to erect
a monument over his grave. But should we before doing
this, let the living object, whom, when dead, we should
thus honour die, without shewing him our gratitude;
then I say, and I say it without sentimentality, that the
very stone we use shall rise up in mutiny against us. I
have not written without a knowledge of the facts that
call forth my remarks. I know that Dr Dick has lived
a long and a laborious life, writing books which have done
much good to man. Should man, therefore, not shew
him good in return ? I know, too, that throughout his life

he has lived with the moderation and meekness of a saint, as he has written with the wisdom of a sage; and knowing these things, I would fain save the country the shame of his becoming a martyr.

I call then, on the public to protect this man. Why does not a body of literay men—with George Gilfillan at their head—without delay, set about this labour of love. We hope, and have faith, that it will at once be done, and be the means of saving the feelings of the friends of this great and good man.

P. L

# POEMS AND SONGS.

# POEMS AND SONGS.

## Sabbath in a Scottish Cottage.

From scenes like these old Scotia's grandeur springs,
That makes her loved at home, revered abroad.

BURNS.

### I.

HAIL! Sabbath morn; welcome sweet day of rest;
Hail to the peaceful joy that comes with thee;
  I love this holy feeling in my breast,
    Which now is caused by all I hear and see.
    Hushed is the din of labour, mute and still
    Is the loud voice of reapers 'mong the corn;
    No more is heard the ploughman whistling shrill,
    The milkmaid's song has ceased, the hunter's horn
Is silent and hung by—all hail to Sabbath morn!

### II.

Soon as the bright sun beams across the lawn,
The humble cottar leaves his lowly bed.
With grateful heart he welcomes in the dawn,
And thanks the GOD who watches o'er his head.

The youngsters soon assemble; and all kneel
Before the Almighty's throne: The father prays;
His words go from the heart to heaven,—all feel
Comfort and peace, and soon their voices raise
In humble notes of joy, of thankfulness and praise.

### III.

And now he takes the Bible—blessed book,
And reads a portion from the Holy Word;
He reads of Joseph's story, and all look
Amazed, whilst listening to the strange record.
He reads of JESUS—God's beloved son,
Who came on earth to wash our sins away;
He reads of what He did—of what was done—
Of what he bore for us by night and day;
His feeling heart is touched, and thus the sire doth say:

### IV.

Lo! Christ our Lord was in a stable born,
And the young babe was in a manger laid;
No pomp, no grandeur, did his birth adorn,
The humble shepherds o'er his body prayed:
He was a man of sorrows and became
Acquainted with our weakness and our woe;
He knew our frailties, and he bore the same
With patience: our rebellious state below
Caused tears of sorrow o'er his sinless cheeks to flow.

## V.

While on this earth he cured the deaf and dumb,
He healed the sick and made the blind to see;
At his command the silent dead did come,
From their dark graves, the captives were set free.
He stilled the raging waters with a word;
He cast out devils—walked upon the sea;
He came to teach mankind to sheath the sword,
To live in peace, and brothers all to be;
Yet man received him not, but pierced him on a tree!

## VI.

They planted on his head a crown of thorns,
And led him forth to Calv'ry there to die.
He bore the cross, and meekly bore the scorns
Of jeering soldiers, and was heard to cry,
My God! My God! and then he closed his eyes
In death. The Temple's vail in twain was riven;
The sun is darkened: Lo, the dead arise:
Huge rocks are rent—men to despair are driven;
And earth affrighted shakes beneath the frown of hea-
    ven.

## VII.

Oh! think on Jesus, think on what he bore,
Obey his word—the sinner's way despise;
Oh! strive to enter in at that straight door,
Which leads to peace for aye beyond the skies.
Remember thy Creator, and in prayer
Implore his aid, then nought hast thou to fear:

Make God your staff and comfort—then though care
Oppress you, when your days are ended here,
A bright beloved saint with Christ you will appear

## VIII.

And thus with them the pleasant moments flow,
The dainties soon are on the table spread,
Of which they all partake, and then they go
To where their father's fathers have been laid—
To the church-yard and the church.   Hark! the
  loud bell
Is pealing through the  wood and o'er the lea;
Now groups are seen on distant hill and dale,
Wending their way with joy to where we see
The spire that points to heaven, in which they hope to be.

## IX.

The guidman and  the  guidwife have each put on
  Their Sunday claes, and seen the bairnies drest;
  Their eldest daughter Jessie, peered by none,
  She too is  buskit in her very best;
And John, their worthy guid respected son—
  Wha toils wi' pleasure for them day by day,
  He wearies not but still he labours on,
  And ne'er an angry word is heard to say—
He is ready for the kirk—his heart is glad  and gay.

## X.

They reach the lone sequestered house of God,
Where friends are loitering in the auld kirk-yard,

Speaking of those who lie beneath the sod,
And heaving sighs o'er friends langsyne interred.
Lo, here the widow weeps her husband lost;
Here the forsaken lonely maid may mourn,
And tell her hapless tale to midnight ghost;
Here wild flowers the green yew tree adorn
The graves of those who sleep till life's eternal morn.

## XI.

The bell has ceased—all enter church, and now
Service begins—a psalm is read and sung:
Their pastor prays: and see on every brow
Sits holy thought at his instructive tongue:
He reads a chapter, then the text is given,
He knows what erring mortals need and want;
He acts and speaks as should a guide to heaven;—
With him there is no hypocritic cant,
No naseous statements made, no raphsody, no rant.

## XII.

He bids them first honour and serve their God,
Love and adore Him, and you will do well;
He bids them strive to gain that blest abode
Beyond the skies, where saints for ever dwell.
He bids them all respect their fellow-men,
And oh, be kind, and feel for others woes;
Be just,—from all dishonest acts refrain,
And the reward is yours.   Peace and repose
Attend the good man still, where'er on earth he goes.

## XIII.

And thus time passes.  Service soon is ended.
The congregation slowly wears away;
Pleasure and joy on every face are blended,—
Oh, they have cause to bless the Sabbath day.
And soon our humble family reach their home,
A lonely cot by whimpling burnie seen:
Meg gi'es them hearty welcome as they come,
Spreads a repast before them a' I ween,
Which  her ain hands prepared, sae wholesome, guid,
    and clean.

## XIV.

A blessing's asked, and then they all partake
That food that God thus gives them day by day—
Again they thank him for his mercy's sake,
And thus the time glides pleasantly away;
The aged father now selects a book
Frae aff his shelves, on which are many seen—
Hail! to those treasures, hail!   But let me look,
What are they ?   ah! the best of books, I ween,
O'er which the earnest student ponders morn and e'en.

## XV.

There's first the big Ha' Bible, and upon
It the good father ponders morn and night—
Then Bunyan's Pilgrim's Progress—honest John
Is read by king and cottar with delight,—
The Four-fold-State by Boston—Watt and Blair,

Stackhouse and Harvey's Mediations too,
Paley and Watson's noble works are there,
Which make the doubting sceptic turn, I trow,
And to his broken reed bid a long last adieu.


## XVI.

There is no blind selection; here are seen
Books on all subjects, art and science too,
Histories of men and nations; and I ween
Of great and gifted poets not a few,—
Shakspeare and Milton, Thomson, Blair, and Burns,
Are kept with care within this humble bield,
And all are read with rapture,—read by turns,
While round the blazing fire or in the field,
Those great and gifted minds unmingled pleasure yield.


## XVII.

But now the sun is sinking in the west,
The day's declining, evening winds grow cool,
The younger cottars now again get dress'd,
For they maun a' gang to the Sabbath school,
The auld guid-wife gets a her young sons near,
To say their tasks to her before they gae;
The guidman gets his daughters, he does speer
Their questions at them ranged around his knee,
He strokes their heads and bids them " say your task
     to me.

## XVII.

And now they leave their humble home, and go
With willing hearts to school, at which are seen
Young groups, all free from sorrow, care, and woe,
With patience loitering on the village green;
And soon they enter, soon their tasks are said;—
Here all are told and taught to sing and pray;
An exhortation's given, a chapter's read,
The young minds made familiar with the way
Of Him who shall appaer at the great Judgment Day.

## XIX.

But time flies on, the twilight bell is pealing,
The sun has sunk behind yon heath-clad hill;
Darkuess on wood and dell is quickly stealing,
Night comes apace and all is hushed and still.—
Homeward in haste our humble group returning
Enter their cot—dispelled is every dread;
The door is barred, the lamp is dimly burning,
The Bible's opened passages are read,
Which, thanks be to our God, console the heart and
    head.

## XX.

Hark! once again the voice of praise ascends;
How the heart melts at melody so sweet!
The contrite bosom in devotion bends,
And yields its grateful homage at the feet
Of him who made the world in which we live;
Who gives us all our comforts day by day,

And sent his Son, who taught us to forgive
Our earthly foes, and pointed out the way
To gain his love who is our comfort, staff, and stay.


## XXI.

Hail! to this humble family, peace and rest
Be ever with them in this world below,—
All hail to him who hath a feeling breast,
Who sees and fain would share a brother's woe;
Peace to the just, the generous, and the good;
Hasten that time, O Lord, when we shall see
Thy holy precepts practised,—understood,—
O then, and not till then, will mankind be
The good and God-like beings meant and made by Thee.

# The Auld Kirk-Yard.

'Tis but night, a long and moonless night,
We make the grave our bed, and then are gone.

BLAIR.

## I.

O! WEEL I like to wander
  When the e'ening sun is set;
When the raven on the castle croaks,
  And the grass wi' dew is wet;
When the birds hae ceased their singin'
  And to their hames repair'd,
Then, O then! I like to wander
  In the auld kirk-yard.

* The small city of the dead that suggested to the author the writing of these lines, is as perfect a ruin as its citizens within; no kind of fence defends it from the raid of the ruthless intruder —yet would the poet reverently linger amongst its stones till the eleventh hour had proclaimed the approach of summer's midnight. About the time it appeared, a friend remarked to the author "that Auld Kirk-Yard seem just an imitation of 'there grows a bonny brier bush in our kail-yard;'" the youth stood some minutes in a state of apparent stupefaction, his face becoming whiter than the paper on which the poem was printed, but at length said "you do not know how much you hurt me; I declare I never saw nor heard of the piece of which you speak. That friend has sometimes since regretted the occurrence; and would say to others similarly situated, do nothing rashly, remember the fate of poor Tannahill.

## II.

In the auld kirk-yard I've pleasures
    That the gay can never hae,
Though whiles I may be gloomy,
    And my heart wi' trouble wae.
O, it's there that I see justice;
    There the cottar and the laird
Lie side by side, and slumber
    In the auld kirk-yard.


## III.

Grim death comes fast upon us,
    And tak's baith ane and a',
He flies about on fiery wing
    And tears our friends awa'.
The father and the mither dies,
    And the bairnie it's no spared,
Folk are freed frae a' their sorrows
    In the auld kirk-yard.


## IV.

I like to see the charnel house,
    Where lie decaying banes;
I like to read the epitaphs
    Engraven on the stanes;
I like to lean upon the tombs,
    And tread the lang green sward,
That waves o'er friends departed,
    In the auld kirk-yard.

E

Here's a nook wi' nae memorial
  Whar the village strangers[*] sleep,
At whose dying hour nae bosom friend
  Was heard to wail or weep.
Here they're laid to rest: nae marbles tell
  The toils on earth they shared;
But their griefs and woes are ended
  In the auld kirk-yard.

## VI.

How aft hae I sat lanely here—
  Nae living mortal wi's—
When a' was dark and dreary,
  And the loud wind 'mang the trees;
I thought on grim ghost stories,
  But e'en then I wasna fear'd,
For I kenn'd that God was wi' me
  In the auld kirk-yard.

## VII.

O, wae's me! what a strange, strange place
  Is this wee spot o' ground—
Sma' though it be, there's mony a true
  And loving heart that's bound

[*] Mr Robert Chambers, in a beautiful essay, speaks thus of
the Stranger's Nook:—' In country church-yards in Scotland,
and perhaps in other countries also, there is always a corner
near the gateway, which is devoted to the reception of strangers,
and is distinguished from the rest of the area, by its total want
of monuments.

To wander here, an' shed sad tears
  O'er friends langsyne interred:
There's something that's enticing
  In the auld kirk-yard.


## VIII.

Still and silent are they sleeping,
  But the day will dawn on graves—
Their inmates shall be roused from death
  And ne'er again be slaves.
The great last day is coming,
  When their God, eternal guard,
Will wake them from their slumber
  In the auld kirk-yard

# My Father's Ha'.

## I.

My Father's Ha'! my Father's Ha'!
  O! I've been happy there,
When sitting round the blazing fire,
  Our hearts sae free frae care.
Despite o' a the ills that came
  To take our peace awa',
We were unco blythe and happy aye
  Around my Father's Ha'.

## II.

I've wandered east, I've wandered west,
  I've wandered 'mang the hills,
And flowery glens and rocky dens,
  And I hae felt the ills
That man on earth is subject to,
  But I hae felt that a';
The cares o' life were banished
  When around my Father's Ha'.

## III.

O! weel I mind the winter nights
  When Boreas blew sae bauld,

When round the ingle cheek we sat
  An' smiled baith young and auld.
We naething had to trouble's then,
  But we heard the loud winds blaw,
An wished the houseless wanderer wi's
  Around my Father's Ha'.


## IV.

It's there that I first learned
  To read guid and holy books,—
It's there that I first saw wi' joy;
  A mither's anxious looks,—
It's there that I first heard the prayer
  Sent up for ane an' a;
It's the sweetest, dearest spot on earth
  To me—my Father's Ha'.


## V.

My Father's Ha', my Father's Ha',
  To me 'twill aye be dear;
An' those wha round it use to sit
  Alas! how few are here.
They're scattered now, and some are to
  A better world awa',
And left us here to think on them
  Around my Faather's Ha'.

## VI.

But we'll a' yet be happy
   When life's journey here is o'er,
We'll meet beyond yon sunny skies,—
   We'll meet to part no more.
Our bliss will be eternal there,
   It will never flee awa';
We'll be happier than we've ever been
   Around my Father's Ha'.

# 7

# Hame Beyond the Skies.

---

## I.

When the heart's oppressed wi' sorrow,
  And the head bowed down wi' care;
When we labour wi' a heavy load
  O' grief and dark despair;
When a' before seems murky,
  And black clouds round us rise,—
It's a blessed thing to think we hae
  A hame beyond the skies.

## II.

When friends wha dearly lo'ed us,
  Wha by us were aye held dear,
When they're lowly laid by fell disease,
  And stretched upon a bier;
When we kiss the cheek sae lately warm,
  And close the glistening eyes—
It's a blessed thing to think we hae
  A hame beyond the skies.

## III.

When our earthly friends forsake us,
  And upon us shut their door,—

When left by a', like some lone tree,
　　Upon a blasted moor,
There's ae friend wha never leaves us,
　　If we're just, and good, and wise,—
It's a blessed thing to think we hae
　　A hame beyond the skies.


### IV.

Ah, me, I often wonder
　　What this weary world would be,
If we kenn'd nae o' anither
　　When in death we closed our e'e;
When we're laid into the lonesome grave,
　　From which we a' maun rise,—
It's a blessed thing to think we hae
　　A hame beyond the skies.


### V.

A' kinds, a' colours, and a' creeds,
　　Are blest wi' hope in heaven;
To saint and savage, Turk and Jew,
　　This balm of life is given.
The Catholic and the Calvanist,
　　Wha ithers' creeds despise,
Think it's a blessed thing to hae
　　A hame beyond the skies.


### VI.

The burdened slave who lives on earth
　　A life of care and woe;

The Greenlander, who climbs o'er hills
   Of everlasting snow;
The poor untutored Indian,
   He who for lack of knowledge dies,
Is taught by nature that he has
   A hame beyond the skies.


## VII.

Let us thank our God, the giver
   Of this cheering hope below,
Which dispels the darkest clouds of fate,
   And sets us free from woe.
There's a land of bliss, where he will wipe
   All tears from weeping eyes,—
It's a blessed thing to think we hae
   A hame beyond the skies.

# Verses to My Aunt.

This is one of my earliest efforts : it will explain itself.   The
person to whom it was written—Mrs Warden of the Plans of
Thornton—is one of the kindest and best of women.   She is one
of " Nature's Nobles," dearly beloved by all who know her.
Would that the world were composed of her like.

## I.

Dearest Aunt, when thinking on your
    Kindness to us day by day,
I see that we are among your
    Debtors wha can never pay.

## II.

When I think upon the ruin
    That comes ower baith ane and a',
When a father wha's weel-doing,
    Frae his family wears awa'.

## III.

When I think, and thinking shiver,
    On the havoc it wad made,
Had my father been forever
    Laid within his narrow bed:

## IV.

When I think upon your kindness
    To him—Aunt, baith air and late,
If my beating heart were mindless,
    Only when it stops to beat.

## V.

A' the toil that you had wi' him,
    Save yourself there's few did see'd;
Still wi' pleasure did you gie him,
    Ilk thing he could wish or need

## VI.

Pale and wan he came out to you—
    Wild disease made dismal strife;
But wi' grace that God did gi'e you,
    You e'en saved his very life.

## VII.

Aft you gaed to pu' at mid day,
    A' the best fruit you could see;
Though he aft to stop did bid you,
    Still you kindly bade him pree.

## VIII.

When the sun had ceased his vigour,
    And in warmth did shine nae mair,
When e'en was calm you placed him
    At the door wi' meikle care.

## IX.

Then he aften saw descending
In the west the setting sun;
Balmy breezes him were mending—
Thus wi' joy the e'en did run.


## X.

At the hour o' midnight, when you
Heard the lonely owlet cry,
You had need of rest; but then—ye
Even then—you couldna lie.


## XI.

Then you'd quietly gae to see him,
And to speer if aught was wrong;
Milk in plenty you did gie him,
Cool'd the almost parched tongue.


## XII.

Dearest Aunt, O can I ever,
Kindness such as that forget?
No! I'm sure that I can never,
Till this heart has ceased to beat.


## XIII.

I, 'tis true, can ne'er reward ye,
Which does fill my heart wi' care;

But accept frae humble bardie,
   A' he has—an earnest prayer.


## XIV.

Peace and pleasure to your cot aye,
   Comfort to the ruling twa;
O, may bliss attend your lot aye—
   Peace to ane, and peace to a'.


## XV·

Comfort to you a' the day-time;
   Peace when laid upon your bed,—
God forsakes the good at nae time,—
   Then he hovers round your head.


## XVI.

When your days on earth are ended,
   When your o'er life's ocean driven,
Cares on earth will a' be mended,
   When you reap the promise given.


## XVII.

Dearest Aunt, I canna gie you
   Words to tell you how I feel;
I maun soon be out to see you—
   God aye bless you—Fare-you-weel!

# The Trysting Tree.

~~~~~~~~~~

### I.

The Trysting Tree! the Trysting Tree!
　　I'll mind it a' my days;
It weel deserves a sang frae me,
　　Or something in its praise.
So sit you doon beside me, love,
　　And I will sing to thee,
The pure delights that we enjoyed
　　Beneath the trysting tree

### II.

D'ye mind when first we met there,
　　I was reading at some book,
When you passed ae summer mornin'
　　An' you gied me sic a look?
Weel I mind you gaed by slowly,
　　An' you seemed to smile to me,—
So I bade you come and rest awhile
　　Beneath the trystin' tree.

### III.

Ye consented and cam near me,
   And, O, Jessie, that ae look
Gar'd me loe ye ever after;
   I loot fa' the very book,—
And I pressed ye to my bosom,
   While the tear stood in my e'e;
Oh, sacred are the joys o' love,
   Beneath the trystin' tree.

### IV.

Beneath the trystin' tree began
   A true love that will last,
Till this fair earth be burned up,
   And all its glories past,—
Yon sun may be extinguished,
   But I'll live and think on thee,
And remember a' the joys we've haen
   Beneath the trystin' tree.

### V.

Yes, the time will come, dear Jessie,
   When e'en you and I maun part,
Oh, ye needna look amazed, nor let
   This touch your tender heart;
For ye ken though death divide us,
   I will meet again with thee,

An hae bliss beyond the joys we've haen
 Beneath the trysting tree .


## VI.

We hae met here ilka e'enin'
 When the eerie bat flew hame;
And we've seen the pale moon gaein
 To that land I canna name;
We hae met here ilka mornin
 Ere the sun cam o'er the sea,
And constant was our happiness
 Beneath the trystin' tree.


## VII.

When wearied nature sank to rest
 An' a' was hushed an' still,
Wi' lightsome heart I crossed the muir,
 An passed the Haunted Mill;✿
The feint a ghaist or bogle
 E'er tried to hinder me,—
I guess they kenn'd they couldna,
 When I sought the trystin' tree.

---

✿ 1741 was a disastrous year for Scotland—had seed and a
backward spring, followed by a wet summer and a late harvest,
brought on the country the evils of famine. At that time (and
not far from the Trysting Tree) there stood, and yet stands, a
Meal-Mill romantically situated on the bank of an ever-running
brook. In a hut, on the farm attached to the mill, there lived a
labourer, having a numerous family and out of work ; he asked

## VIII.

O, it's here I vowed to lo'e you
   While my life was spared below
Here I vowed to shield and guard you
   Frae this warld's care and woe;
It's here at'times we baith hae prayed
   Upon the bended knee,—
We've tasted bliss beyond compare
   Beneath the trystin' tree

from the miller (on credit) a small quantity of meal: the favour was refused; the family was starving; and driven to desperation by their cries for bread, in the course of the night, he went to the mill, and getting in by a wide aperture in the wall, through which passed the axle of the wheel, was in the act of filling a bag with meal, when unfortunately for him the miller entered, with a light in his hand, for the purpose of setting on the mill. Being thus detected, the miller took him to the house, where a fire was already blazing on the hearth, upon which was a heated girdle for the purpose of firing the bread which the servants were baking for the family's use. Either from infatuation or frolic it was agreed—that as his feet had brought him to the mill, and as his hands had stolen the meal—to place all four on the red-hot girdle; which they accordingly did with great violence, his agony and cries for mercy being of none avail. A female relative of the miller's cried out 'dinna let him go till I put in anither cowe yet.' Getting at last released, he crawled out on his elbows and knees, until he reached the cart shed, where death ere long put an end to his sufferings. The man being poor, the miller's influence prevailed, and the affair was therefore hushed over. The mill was ever after said to be haunted. The miller's family is now extinct; their affairs having previously gone to ruin; and not a few of them suffered violent deaths. To this time, if the neighbours have to go that way at night, they generally feel timorous as they pass the haunted mill.

## IX.

Here I rowed you in my plaidie,
　　Frae the cauld and biting blast,
Though the trysting tree can shield us,
　　Frae the north wind or the wast;
I bound a wreath around your brow,
　　A token true to thee,
That we were bound in bands o' love
　　Beneath the trystin' tree.

## X.

When I think on the days, Jessie,
　　My fond heart is like to break;
But I stop the tears, for weel I ken
　　That her for wha's dear sake
I sigh, still lo'es me fondly;
　　Still is fondly lo'ed by me,—
And our first affection was begun
　　Beneath the trystin' tree.

## XI.

D'ye ye mind that time, dear lassie,
　　When I left ye to yoursel',
I'm sure we baith had sorrows which
　　Nae tongue can ever tell.
I came and waited though I kenn'd
　　I wadna meet wi' thee;
Oh, I thought my very heart would break
　　Beneath the trystin' tree.

## XII.

When winter comes, our trystin' tree
   Grows naked, brown, and bare;
Like mother Nature round about,
   It hangs its head wi' care.
But spring returns and it revives,
   As ye may plainly see,—
There's no a tree about a the burn
   Like our ain trystin' tree.

# 8

# Man to Peace was Born.

In imitation of " MAN WAS MADE TO MOURN. "

## I.

When gentle spring's ethereal bloom
　　Made fields and forests gay,
One morning as 1 wandered forth
　　Along the banks of Tay,
I spied a man whose back was bent,
　　But cankering grief and care
Seemed utter strangers to his heart,
　　Though hoary was his his hair

## II.

Young stranger, whither wanderest thou?
　　Began the reverend sage;
Does love of nature call thee forth,
　　Before bowed down with age?
Or haply wilt thou talk with me
　　Of providence's plan,
And vindicate the ways of God
　　To noble-minded man.

## III.

Yon sun, that sheds a golden flood
    Of light on tower and tree,
And tells us there's a God above,
    Delights and pleases me.
I've seen yon glorious brilliant sun
    Twice forty times return,
And every time has added proof
    That man to peace was born.

## IV.

My son, when young be wise—be not
    Too prodigal of time;
Do not misspend thy precious hours,
    Thy glorious youthful prime.
O, let not follies take their sway,
    Do not let passions burn,—
Curb and contemn them, e'en to-day,
    And then thou wilt not mourn.

## V.

'Tis true that tyrants, while in power
    Oppress man here below;
But why from this should it be said,
    That man was doomed to woe.
'Tis madness for the rich and great
    To treat the poor with scorn;

Oh, why has man the will and power
  To make his fellow mourn.


## VI.

Were mankind wise, we all might be
  In pleasure's lap caressed,—
There's plenty here for high and low,
  To make us truly blest;
But sordid, sinful, selfish men,
  Hoard up all that they can,
And while they only serve themselves,
  Oppress their fellow men.


## VII.

Many and sharp the numerous ills
  Inwoven with our frame,
And oft we cause remorse and grief
  By bringing on the same.
Oh, were mankind, when young, all taught
  The wicked's path to scorn,
Then blest experience soon would show
  That man to peace was born


## VIII.

See yonder ploughman on the field,
  He whistles as he goes;

He knows not grief, nor care—his heart
  Is ne'er oppressed with woes.
And when at e'en his toil is o'er
  He homeward doth return,
Lo! there he meets a cheerful wife,
  And babes to bless him born.


## IX.

Proud man to be a slave was ne'er
  By nature's law designed,
Then why should weak and puny man
  To earth his brother bind?
Oh! shake the fetters from the feet
  Of slaves; wipe off this scorn
And just reproach from nature; show
  To freedom man was born.


## X.

Yet, let not this too much, my son,
  Engage thy youthful breast;
Think not this world's a paradise;
  Perhaps indeed 'twere best
To think and to believe that we
  Are happy here below;
But, only if we're just and good;
  If not we dwell in woe.

## XI.

Death is the good man's greatest friend,
 The kindest and the best;
For then his toils are at an end—
 He's taken to his rest.
The vile and wicked fear its blow,
 From sin to sorrow torn;
But the just and good ne'er fear to go
 Who know for what they're born.

# Martha Palmer.

---

### I.

Oh, dear, dear Martha Palmer,
  A' the grief you've gien to me,
It's far beyond my humble power
  In words to tell to thee;
But my heart's sae fu' o' sorrow
  At the change I've lately seen,
That I canna do but tell you o't,
  And ask what ye could mean.

### II.

I little thought that slanders, love,
  Of heartless envious men,
Could e'er hae poison'd your high mind,
  Or made you false; but then
I find the love of woman
  Is a frail and quivering reed,
And the heart that doats too fondly,
  Is the heart that doats to bleed.

G

### III.

D'ye mind the scenes that we twa had
    Since first we met th'gither;
D'ye mind the vows we made, to live
    In love wi' ane anither;
D'ye mind the tears we aften shed,
    For very bliss and joy,—
Did you think then, Martha, did you m·
    Our rapture to destroy?

### IV.

Oh! how aften did we wander
    When the sun sunk o'er the hill,
Down the saugh road, across the burn,
    An' by the haunted mill,
Up to the kirk and auld kirk-yard,
    Which ye would scarcely leave,—
For weel you lo'ed to linger
    By the murdered martyr's grave.

### V.

Whiles when we stood frae wind or rain,
    Beside the auld grey tower,
An' saw the pale moon glimmering
    At the solemn midnight hour.
I told you warlock stories,
    And I've felt you cling to me,

As if I were your salvation,—
  Which indeed I weel could be.


## VI.

And ah, we aften sat, my dear,
  Beneath the trystin' tree,
Where I made love to you, my dear,
  An' you made love to me,
An' when we baith were left alane,
  An' nae intruder near,
We spoke the poems and sung the sangs,
  That true hearts like to hear.


## VII.

Ah then, dear Martha, then this earth
  Was paradise to me!
This heart, sae heavy now, was light
  When I was lo'ed by thee.
The flowers were bonnie, fields were green,
  Frae ilka bush and tree
The birds sang sweetly, very sweet,
  When Martha smiled on me.


## VIII.

But now that you hae left me,
  Now that we by fate are parted;
Now that you hae sought to live alane,
  And I am broken hearted,—

I see not nature as it was;
 The earth, the sun, the sea,
The trees, the birds. the bonnie flowers,
 Are naething now to me.


## IX.

At midnight like a ghaist I gang;
 And love, 'tween you and me,
I've fearfu' thoughts o' something,
 Which I darena tell to thee.
I weep whiles like a very child,
 For a' my hopes are hurl'd
To fell destruction, and I'm left
 Alane in this dark world.


## X.

You, dearest, have the triumph
 Of disdaining slighting me;
But I would not boast of glory,
 Had I done the same to thee.
True love should not be scorned;
 It is sent to earth from heaven,
As the purest and the rarest gift
 That God to man hath given,


## XI.

Fareweel, dear Martha, you may ne er
 Forget me a' th'gether;

And I ken you'll keep your aith to God,
   That you'll ne'er wed anither.
If it be sae, I know that when
   Frae earth we gang awa',
I'll meet you in a better world,
   As pure as winter snaw.

# A Welcome to Queen Victoria and Prince Albert,

ON THEIR VISIT TO DUNDEE.

---

The following Verses were sent to the Queen, during her residence at Blair Castle, through her Foreign Secretary, the Earl of Aberdeen. His Lordship was kind enough to send me a note acknowledging the receipt of the Poem by her Majesty.

---

"Stir the beal-fire—wave the banner—
  Bid the thundering cannon sound,
Rend the skies with acclamation,
  Stun the woods and water round,
Till the echoes of our gathering
  Turn the world's admiring gaze,
To this act of duteous homage
  Scotland to VICTORIA pays."

DELTA.

---

## I.

DUNDEE welcomes with kind greeting,
  Fair Victoria to our shore;
And we hail the Queen of Nations
  Whom we honour and adore;
And we hail her joyful Consort,
  Worthy of her fondest love,—
May their days on earth be happy,
  Till they reach the land above.

## II.

Thou bright sun! beam forth in splendour—
   Shine out on the royal pair—
Rise our beating hearts and let us
   Bid a long adieu to care.
For this the day and this the hour,
   With heartfelt joy we see,
Britain's great and peerless Queen
   In our native home Dundee.

## III.

Lo, the lofty arch triumphal,
   Rears it columns to the skies,—
Widely open'd be its portals
   To our Queen's admiring eyes.
The cannons sound—the banners wave—
   The fairest flowers are seen
All bound in wreaths right royally—
   To welcome Albion's Queen.

## IV.

We would wish that this their visit
   In auld loyal Scotland, be
Marked by all that kindly feeling,
   Which is ever with the free!
We would wish them to be happy
   While in Scotia they remain;

And may ever joy attend them
　　To the " merry " land again.


### V.

May their sports among the heather
　　Be what bounding hearts desire,
May the hills, and glens, and fountains,
　　Them with health and mirth inspire.
Let us welcome Queen Victoria
　　To her Highland home with glee,
Where the heathcock's screaming loudly
　　And the wild dear bounding free.


### VI.

May the reign of Queen Victoria,
　　Be a reign of rest and peace,
Prompted by her bright example,
　　May all strife and discord cease.
May her ministers act wisely,
　　And may all her subjects be
Ever loving—ever loyal—
　　Ever fearless, bold, and free.


### VII.

May the royal babes be happy,
　　Till their parents home return,
In their own loved land, O, may they
　　Ne'er have cause to grieve or mourn

May they grow in grace and beauty;
 May they ever, ever prove
Choicest blessings to their parents,
 Who reward them with their love.


## VIII.

So we welcome here Prince Albert,
 Consort to our Royal Queen,—
May his days on earth be happy,
 As his days gone by have been !
And we welcome with kind greeting
 Fair Victoria to our shore;
And we hail the Queen of Nations
 Whom we honour and adore.

# The Kirk.

'Twas Sabbath e'en, the setting sun
   Out o'er the Law* was glowering;
The day o' rest was nearly done,
   And night's dark clouds were lowering.

The golden west I gladly saw
   Were by the sun's rays riven;
At length he calmly sunk away,—
   Like saint that soars to heaven.


As I stood, and wi' pleasure gazed
   Upon the face of nature,
I saw what made me much amazed—
   A maid wha's every feature,

Betokened that she had not been
   A dweller 'mang the rest o's,
For baith her mannor and her mien
   Was better than the best o's,

---

\* The *Law*, a notable hill behind Dundee, containing on its
summit the remains of a Roman Fortress.

Wi' smiling face she took my hand,
   And pointing up to heaven,
Said, " Sir, that is the happy land,
   There bliss to all is given."


She smiled again, " Dear Sir," said she,
   " My name is Guide to Glory;
O come wi' me I'll let you see
   A scene at which I'm sorry."


I bow'd, and kissed her bonny hand,
   Then on wi' joy she led me,
An' aft to seek the happy land,
   Wi' smiling face she bade me.


She led me to the kirk, where I
   Hae aften heard a sermon;
But, guid forgie me when I say
   We landed 'mang a vermin.


" Now, Sir, I've brought you here, you se'
   'Mong mony lads and lasses;
Sit down and tell the world and me,
   The scenes that 'mang them passes.


"And Oh," said she, her hand up high,
   " Do a' as I would hae you;"
Then round my brow a wreath did tie—
   " May that and God be wi' you."

Soon as these kind words she said,
　She frae my sight was hidden;
I prayed to God to bless the maid,
　Then strove to do her bidding.


His reverence soon came up the stair,
　And vow but there's a reaching
O' heads and caps—it's a' the care
　O' some to see wha's preaching.


For mony a ane I ween is there
　Wha to the text will listen;
When this is got they dinna care
　For sermon or for blessing.


I kenna what the kimmer means,—
　She s doing aught but looking,
The trifling brat's but in her teens,
　And watch her how she is poking


Her neebour's ribs, saying "'cast your e'e
　Out ower amang the fellows,
And if a wise-like chield you see,
　You'll no forget to tell us."


Should some late comer want a seat,
　And scarce ken whar to find ane;
Some bonny quean will no be blate
　To crush and prove a kind ane;

And a' the pay for favour shown,
　　Or fee she seeks frae him,
Is just to get his arm when done,
　　And take a dander wi' him.


I cast my e'e across the kirk
　　Whar folk should aye sit douse;
A rotten seat came down wi' jerk,
　　And this creates a noise.


It put the maist o' folk on edge;—
　　And yonder's three chields brisk aye;
See, Tam's now in an awfu' rage,
　　For Bob's drunk a' the whisky.


A modest matron sitting douse
　　Was for some minutes pested;
She thought that 'mang her feet a mouse,
　　Was jumping, but to test it,


She soon resolved inspite o' a',
　　She would be at the meaning,—
Sae looking down I ween she saw,
　　A fellow busy preening


Her petticoats; but weel I wat
　　The kind chield got a to' en,—
The matron rose to stand, wi' that
　　The gallant's joke was broken.

H

Look ye up yonder! there's three chiels,
  At " catch the ten " they're playing,
And hear yon callant how  he bans
  At what his neebour's saying.


And round and round are maids and men,
  Quite the reverse o' civil;
They make the house o' God a den
  In which to do a' evil.


Where is the genius of those rules,
  Those precepts that would ease us,—
Where are the teachers of those schools
  Begun on earth  by Jesus?

# Stubb's Fair.

### I.

" Come, Pate, gie't ower man, work nae mair,
Let's baith gae out and see the fair,
  Ilk lightsome body's fleeing;
The road I see is thickly clad,
Wi' mony a bonny lass and lad,
  They'll a' be worth the seeing;''
So said my friend, and quickly then
  I rose and took the road,
On which were droves o' merry men,
  And lasses neat and snod,—
And a' that I saw,
  As I here and there was driven,
Just proved ilka ane loved
  To be lightsome as weel's livin'.

### II.

And mony a ploughman chield was seen
Wha that night got rowin e'en,
  And some could scarcely stand.

I like a chield right glad to be,
Whene'er he meets wi' twa or three,
　　To grip hard friendship's hand.
I aften ower a hearty stoup,
　　Hae spent a happy night,
But it's far the best and wisest plan
　　To keep ane's sell near right.
It's beastly—I maistly
　　Could ca' the fellow down,
Wha sits till his wits
　　Wi' the warld's rinning round.


### III.

There's mony a poor thing on the road
This day hae left their sad abode;
　　And waes me they maun beg.
Wives, wed to poortith, wi' a bairn,
And mony a man without the arm,
　　And some without a leg:
I like to see a generous chiel,
　　Wi' open liberal hand,
It shows I ween his heart can feel
　　For this neglected band,
To gie what he'll see that
　　To him will ne'er be missing:
I like to hear wi' listening ear,
　　The poor auld beggar's blessing


### IV.

Hark to those sounds from yonder tent,
I'm sure there's some ane discontent;

Although I wadna wish't.
Alas my friend, what can it be ?
The lads wi' scarlet coats, you see,
　　Are wanting Will to list.
"Man, Will, how can you gang awa'
　　Frae hame and friends sae far ?"
Said Rodger " can you leave us a',
　　To face the waes o' war,
Man, Willie, be nae silly;
　　Dinna plunge to sic a fate—
I'll no deceive, but me believe,
　　You'll rue't when far ower late."

### V.

Says　Will " my friend I ken you weel;
I ken that much for me yon feel;
　　But here believe me, Rodger,
I'm gaun to do't—yes, here I'm willing
The minute that I get the shilling
　　To gae and be a sodger.
And as for her the saucy fair—
　　My mind is on the rack—
She slighted me, but here I swear
　　I'll pay the false ane back;
So, Roger, here I vow and swear
　　To leave ilk social chiel',
To ilka brae and ilka burn,
　　To ane and a' fareweel."

### VI.

Poor senseless Will the shilling got,
The sergeant called the tither pot,

And cried " Our friend will pay't."
The beer was brought, round went the drink—
Will's spirits soon began to sink,
   They wi' his shilling gaed.
" Come, do not let your spirits down,"
   The winning soldier said;
" Cheer up, my lad, and do not fear,
   A man you'll soon be made."
He cried then and dried then
   The tears that down did fa',
The daft ane, the saft ane,
   Was easily won awa'.

### VII.

And list again to that loud noise
Of drums and fifes, and men, and boys;
   Observe ye, these are players,—
They surely lead an awfu' life,
Of toil and trouble, strut and strife,
   Of crosses and of cares,
They're pinched, I wat, by poverty,
   And naked maist for claes;
Thus strolling through the world they gae
   And spend their weary days.
Nae hame can they claim,
   And nae comfort can they have;
They're hurl'd through the world,
   Till they sink into the grave.

### VIII.

And mony a kittle case was seen,
   Wi' hearty Jock and rosy Jean;

I wat he gart her reel;
And kindness came at ilka hand,
He treated her at tent and stand,
  And pleased the lassie weel.
And mony a chapman chield was there,
  Wi' ranting roaring voice,
Some selling saft and some hard ware,
  A penny for your choice.
And a' that I saw,
  As I here and there was driven,
Just proved ilk ane loved
  To be lightsome as weel as livin'.

# The Murdered Fly.

## I.

I once lived in a cottage,
  And its master prayed and sung;
Every morning, every evening,
  This little mansion rung.
I had thought that he was holy,
  But if such thought be true,
You may juge when I've related
  What once happened to my view.

## II.

One summer morning early,
  I beheld my host's young daughter
Catch a little fly, and first
  She put it in a jug of water;
She took it out, tore both its wings,
  And beat it every part;
Said I has this young child been taught
  The feelings of the heart.

### III.

I beheld her still—for now to save
    The fly was all in vain—
So she put it on a stone
    And beat it o'er and o'er again;
She bruised and ground it so
    That it was truly out of sight,
Then she rose, ran to her playmates,
    And laughed in pure delight.


### IV.

Now I thought on what had happened,
    And I thought upon the father,
And I thought instead of tame dull prayers
    This holy man should rather
Take his little child and teach her
    What is right and what is wrong
He was bade do so, but never bade
    By holy prayer and song.


### V.

As it now is her heart will be
    A rank unweeded garden;
The things there gross will grow,
    And she in crime will harden.
The mind which God had gifted, lost,
    Time, talents thrown away;
It were well would parents profit
    From the scene I saw to-day.

# The Miseries of War.

---

## I.

AMONG the many visitants, since first the world began,
That have come on earth to murder and destroy the
peace of man.
I stand alone, and go beyond all other ills as far
As the brilliant sun of summer goes beyond the morning
star.

## II.

I have fatted all the fields of earth with the bodies of the
dead;
I have made your crystal streamlets and your rivers all
run red;
And the bravest and the best of men I've buried in the
deep,
Whose dying groans were heard in heaven, and made the
angels weep.

### III.

I have brought destruction on the world, where gorgeous
    cities stood,
Their temples, towers, and palaces I've mingled with the
    blood.
Of fallen men, I've marred earth's joys, and with my
    fiery rod
I've made this world a charnel house for the erring sons
    of God.

### IV.

I have dragged from many a happy home the parents' joy
    and pride,
And I've torn the loving husband from the new-made
    mother's side,
With fiendish joy I led them to the bloody battle plain,
Where the music of my madness was the wailing o'er the
    slain.

### V.

My food hath been the flesh of men, my drink hath been
    their blood,
Give me murdered men or murderers, whether by field
    or flood;
The thundering cannon, glancing steel, and carnage
    covered field,
Murder and death to me a joy uspeakable did yield.

## VI.

I come from hell the deepest hell; this world that would
    be fair,
Were it not for me, I've filled with dismal howlings of
    despair;
If one had been "the hero of an hundred fights or more
I'm the hero of ten million miseries, counted o'er and o'er.

## VII.

I've had friends on earth, and my most favoured son of
    modern times,
Whose deeds heroic, erring poets have sung in lofty
    rhymes,
He was banished on a lonely rock in solitude to dwell,
And the men who wanted peace on earth in doing this
    did well.

## VIII.

Ye nations of the earth give earthink on the deeds I've
    done,
Think on the rendings of the heart, the woes by battle
    won,
Think on the pangs of dying men whose sufferings now
    are o'er;
You may think on this, but ye who suffer not, can do
    no more.

## IX.

Ho, England, France, America! shake hands and live in
    peace,
Put up your swords, ye sons of men, let strife and discord
    cease;
Thou boasted Briton, sun burnt Moor, ye great on earth
    and small,
Love while you live, ye brethren, as God meant and
    made you all.

## X.

I'm getting old and wrinkled now, my hair is turning
    grey,
The world begins to like me less; there dawns a brighter
    day.
I've done my work—I'm wishing that my reign on earth
    was o'er;
For I'm wearied with the deeds I've done and wish to do
    no more.

# Verses

*Written on visiting the Graves of Alexander and John Bethune.*

---

Alexander and John Bethune were brothers. They were born at Upper Rankeillour, in the parish of Letham, and county of Fife. Being the sons of poor parents, they were trained from their earliest days to win their bread by labour. Through life they had to struggle with poverty; during the day they laboured and at night and other limited leisure hours, they wrote poems and stories which attracted the attention of very eminent literary characters ; Mr Murray and Mr R. Chambers being among their patrons. From Woodmill, in the parish of Abdie, they ultimately removed to Mount Pleasant, where Alexander and John had built a house, which will long remain as a monumen of their industry and perseverance It stands on a lofty hill, and is the highest house at the back of the beautiful town of New-burgh. Here the family lived for some time, but death came upon them, and his shafts flew quick. The father died first, then John, then the mother, and Alexander, who was left alone in this, to him, "bleak world," soon followed them to the grave, and now they all rest in the Abdie churchyard, where a chaste and beautiful monument tells who lie below.

In the spring of 1845, I spent a few days at Newburgh. During my stay, I was favoured by a friend with Mr Combie's deeply interesting memoirs of Alexander. I had heard much of the Bethunes before this ; but being in the locality where they had lived and died, and reading this ably compiled work, my in-terest in them was excited, and I had an ardent desire to see the burial place of the brothers. Accordingly, I set out on a Sabbath evening to Abdie churchyard, and it was to me a delightful evening—such a one, indeed, as memory "will not willingly let die." I was enchanted by all I heard and saw. The scenery agreeably surprised me. It was unlooked for. I did not think there was so much beauty in the locality so little talked of Around me lay the hills, reposing in quiet grandeur, and before

me lay the Loch of Lindores, bounded on the north by the beauti-
ful seat of Captain (afterwards Admiral) Maitland, to whom
Napoleon Bonaparte surrendered, off Rochfort, after the battle of
Waterloo, " Which n the calm twillight of a summer's evening
appears like the eye of nature, looking up to its maker in the
spirit of meek and quiet devotion." I arrived at Abdie church-
yard, and standing over the grave of departed genius, the follow-
ing verses were written.

## I.

Rest in peace, beloved brothers—
    Rest in peace, oppressed no more;
Fame is yours which was no other's,
    Now that all life's toils are o'er.

## II.

Bred 'mid hardship, shame upon her,
    Tho' she strove to keep you down,
You have gained a name of honour
    Brighter far than monarch's crown.

## III.

Toiled from morning's sun till setting—
    Students pale o'er glimmering lamp,
Still harassed by fortune fretting—
    Murdered in a cottage damp.

## VI.

Told in your affecting stories,
    What was right and what was wrong;

When inspired by nature's glories
   Then your souls burst forth in song.

## V.

Both were peasants, proud yet humble,
   To their lowly lot resigned;
Neither at their fate did grumble—
   Gifted each with noble mind.

## VI.

Both were one in fond affection—
   One in feeling—one in faith;
One too in their name's erection—
   One in life, and one in death.

## VII.

Standing here, I am not weeping
   O'er their graves now free from ills;
Buried here, serenely sleeping
   'Mid auld Scotia's quiet hills,

## VIII.

Standing here, I do not mourn
   O'er this lowly bed of thine—
Oh! till death's eternal morn,
   May such bed of rest be mine.

## IX.

Here all lie, the father, mother,
　Silently are sleeping here;
Here the younger, elder brother,
　Both are stretched upon the bier.


## X.

Be it so; they all resided
　In one cot on earth in love;
And they were not long divided
　From the better land above.


## XI.

Pilgrims here with bosoms swelling
　Yet may come; and tears may fall
O'er the dark and narrow dwelling
　Of two brothers—one in all.


## XII.

Rest in peace, beloved brothers—
　Rest in peace, oppressed no more;
Fame is yours which was no others,
　Now that all life's toils are o'er.

# The Wind.

## I.

I DINNA like that dreary wind
  It makes me dull and wae;
It gars me think upon the grave,
  To which we a' maun gae.
It brings me to the gates of death
  Whar a' is dark and drear—
There's something in the howling wind
  I dinna like to hear.

## II

It brings to mind the tales I've read,
  O' mountain, moor, and glen,
Where solitary wanderers found
  Remains of murdered men.
I think upon the houseless poor
  Wha wander wet and cauld;
And sigh for a' the sufferings
  O' the helpless young and auld.

## III.

Hark! how that gust is howling,
  Oh, it makes my blood run chill;
What a dreary sound gangs through the trees,
  It's moaning o'er the hill.

Grim sprites arise, and lo! methinks,
  Right merrily behind
The charnel house they're dancing
  To the music of the wind.


## IV.

Ye howling winds, oh, spare the bark,
  On restless billows tossed;
And spare the worthy father
  Deem'd by friends forever lost;
And spare me a' the gloomy thoughts
  That make me shake wi fear,
There's something in the howling wind
  I dinna like to hear.'

# Prologue

---

WELCOME to Stony Knolls! a hearty greeting
We give to all at this our joyful meeting.
Not, it is true, the FIRST, for there have been
Such bright assemblies here before, I ween.
And judging from the glories of the past
I know not, friends, that this should be our LAST,
Shakspeare has said that " all the world's a stage;
" Tis said this is the saying of a sage"
Full well we know 'tis true, but in this mart
Of learning we have mostly played one part—
" The school-boy with his shining morning face
Plays here his part—to him a serious case.
Here day by day, and week by week,
Are dull brains cudgelled over puzzling Greek;
Eutopius teases here, and Virgil vexes,
Horace is horrible,—Euclid perplexes.
Here British commerce, textile manufacture,
Are themes on which we show ourselvesthe actor.
While sums, and numbers added to the sum,
Are themes on which our actors oft prove dumb;
And this truth is told in many a serious look,

That "Latin made Easy,' is no easy book.
Change is the law of nature. Change has been
Since first Creation's dawn beheld the queen
Of earth and women:—pardon, ladies all,
I speak of Eve anterior to her fall.
Since then, the great and everlasting sea
Has sung its wild and endless melody.
The beauteous flowers of summer yearly blow,
Anon comes surly winter with its snow.
Change rules the varied year, the life of man,
And woman, too, though bounded by a span;
So, from the ills with which we have to fight,
We wished to have a change and so, "quite right,"
Exclaimed our actors all, and thus the ending
Of this shrewd thought is what just now is pending.
Thus have we left the Gods of Greek and Rome,
And for one night at least become the showman.
Well, for our own amusement and yours, we
Have chosen the Critic, which you soon will see;
The Spoiled Child,—by the way, offence to none,
We hope that in our temple there's but one;—
And Monsieur Tonson, with his tricks and fun,
With which the night's amusement will be done.
Here great Macready will not tread the stage,
Nor Vandenhoff the grand your time engage.
Here G. V. Brooke, 'tis true, will not be seen,
Nor Helen Faucit, tragedy's fair queen.
But here's *Miss Beard,* of whom the Greeks would say
Her the Gods love to honour and obey:
Here's *Kriens,* to treat us to a German song
He cannot chant too often and too long:
*Moses,* with all his learning too, is here,

To show his talent in another sphere.

Here's *David Slater* playing the greatest part,
Because most like to steal a lady's heart:
Here's *Edwin Smith, alias* Socrates,
Having at once the power and will to please;
Here's *Blacket*, too, with all his fun and tricks,
To act, as he himself would say " like bricks."
These will be seen, and many more besides;
So, laughter, now prepare to hold your sides.
We'll do our best—if high we cannot soar—
Macready or Vandenhoff could do no more.

# SONGS.

## Whar are a' the Friends?

Air,—" O, why left I my hame.'

### I.

Oh! whar are a' the friends
  I had in early days?
Wha used to sport about
  The burnies and the braes;
Wha used to sport about,
  Wi' meikle mirth and glee;
I ween they a' hae fled
  Frae their ain countrie.

### II.

The sangs they used to sing
  Are never heard ava;
The village ne'er docs ring
  Wi' the fife or bugle's blaw;—
It's true that some are laid
  Beyond yon auld yew tree;
But maist o' them are fled
  Frae their ain countrie.

### III.

At kirk or market noo
    We never meet them there;
It makes me wae to think
    I ne'er may see them mair.
We ne'er assemble now
    Our village sports to see;
A's dull and lonely now
    In our ain countrie.

### IV.

My friends are far awa',
    They're scattered here an' there:
But O, for ane and a'
    I breathe this earnest prayer.—
May God still be their guide,
    Wherever they may be,—
May peace and rest be their's
    In anither countrie.

---

## Oh! Here Lies low the Bonny Lass.

AIR—" Oh! where, and oh where?"

### I.

Oh! here lies low the bonny lass,
    The maiden that I lo'e;
She lies within this narrow bed,
    Where I maun soon lie too;

Death's clay cauld hand has stilled the heart,
  That aye was kind and true;
The form o'er which I fondly hung
  Is sheltered by the yew.


## II.

The flowers bloom bonny o'er the bed
  O' her that I held dear;
And dark, dark, is the envious grave
  That keeps me mourning here.
I've naebody noo to live for,
  And the warld's nought to me
Oh, life's a weary pilgrimage,
  My Mary, wanting thee.


## III.

Pale, pale, forever are those lips
  That I hae aften kissed;
And cauld forever are those cheeks
  That I hae aften pressed;
And still forever is that voice,
  Once music to my ear;
Those beaming eyes that shone so bright
  Are closed forever here.


## IV.

O, may I know this blissful home,
  In which my love doth dwell,

K

In yon bright land where happy ones
   Their holy anthems swell;
Where saints forever sing their songs
   To God who reigns on high,
Where sorrow never more is known,
   Nor tears bedim the eye.


### V.

But I am alone on earth,
   My grief I cannot hide;
And I will ne'er find peace or rest
   Till slumbering by her side;
Till then, my beating heart, be still,
   Which now in sorrow lies,—
Oh! I maun soon be blest wi' her
   Beyond yon sunny skies.

---

## When thinking upon My Sad Fate.

AIR,—'My Lass's Black E'e.'

### I.

When thinking upon my sad fate, wi' my Annie,
   This bosom o' mine it is burdened wi' care;
There's something within tells me plain that I maun
   Think I can get peace to my soul ony mair.

## II.

I think that there's nane o' her kind half sae bonny,
   There's nane o' her kind half sae bonny can be;
Her face it is fairer, far fairer than ony,
   Her form it seems like an angel's to me.


## III.

Sometimes in my fondness, when on her I'm thinking,
   I stand and look down wi' the tear in my e'e,
I find my wae heart in my bosom aye sinking,
   Then start, quite regardless wherever I gae.


## IV.

I start, but the wound in my bosom is biding—
   Ah! meikle I fear it will ne'er gang awa;
And though a' my grief frae my friends I am hiding,
   The cauld hand o' death will devour and tell a'.

---

## Hill and Dell are Decked in Green.

Air—'Gloomy Winter.'

### I.

Hill and dell are decked in green,—
Nature's a' in beauty seen;
Il'k thing delights my gazing een;
   And so does lovely Annie, O.

## II.

By yon burn the daisies spring,
On yon bower the birdies sing,
They joy to every bosom bring,
   And sae does lovely Annie, O.

## III.

Wha could now be sad or wae,
When nature a' is blythe and gay?
Tis I, because I dinna hae
   The heart o' lovely Annie, O.

## IV.

I maun wander here and mourn,—
She has slighted me with scorn,
And left me here alane forlorn,—
   My ain lovely Annie, O.

## V.

What are nature's joys to me ?
What her pleasures,—wanting thee
Happy I can never be,
   Unless wi' lovely Annie, O.

## VI.

Will ye, bonny lass, be true ?
Will ye listen to my vow ?
And I will ne'er be false to you,
   My ain, my lovely Annie, O.

# I Now Maun Leave My Lady Fair.

## I.

I now maun leave my lady fair;
　　The wind blows high —the boat is ready,
The boat that fills my heart wi' care,
　　An' bears me frae my winsome lady.
Oh, sair, sair, is this waefu' heart,
　　An' fain, fain would I langer tarry;
But fate has said that we maun part,
　　An' I maun leave my bonny Mary.

## II.

I needna say her heart is true—
　　I needna say she is fair and bonny;
For maist fouk think her matched by few,
　　She is fairer far than ony.
I needna say our love will last
　　Till baith our een are closed forever;
But ah, I fear the joys now past
　　Will never come again—oh, never.

## III.

It's no her e'en sae bonny blue,—
　　It's no her cheek sae red and rosy,
That gars me greet to say adieu,—
　　It's no her fond embrace, sae cosy.

It's no that I regret to leave
 The humble cot in which she's dwelling—
It's no for fear that she'll deceive—
 It's no for this my bosom's swelling.

### IV.

But it's to leave her all alone,
 A lovely maiden unprotected;
Oh! who will gaurd her when I'm gone,
 By me she ne'er wad be neglected.
The power aboon keep watch and care
 O' worth and merit—He'll reward her.
This aye will be my earnest prayer—
 May a' that's guid forever guard her!

---

## Come to Yonder Bower.

---

### I.

Come to yonder bower, my lassie,
 Come to yonder bower wi' me,—
Come to yonder bower, my lassie,
 There I'll tell my love to thee.

### II.

Down by yonder wood, my lassie,
 Blythly a' the birdies sing,
And upon the burnie's banks,
 Roses fair and lilies spring.

### III.

O'er the eastern hill, my lassie,
  Blythly blinks the rising sun;
Hark, the birds aboon our heads,
  Mornings joy's are just begun.

### IV.

What are a' the joys, my lassie,
  That smiling morn can gie,—
What are a' the joys, my lassie,
  Nought, believe me, wanting thee.

---

# Winter Nights are Cauld.

### I

Winter nights are cauld lassie;
  Winter nights are cauld, lassie;
Come my love, O, come wi' me,
  When Boreas' blast is bauld, lassie.

### II.

I've a couthie hame, laddie,
  I've a couthie hame, laddie;
I've my father's humble roof,
  Except me he has nane, laddie.

### III.

I'll keep him trig an' braw, lassie,
   I'll keep him trig an' braw, lassie;
About your parents dinna fear,
   But wi' me come awa, lassie.

### IV.

Gin summer time were here, laddie,
   Gin summer time were here, laddie,
Then, O then, I'll come wi' thee;—
   Just gie me time to speer, laddie.

### V.

I canna bide my lane, lassie,
   I canna bide my lane, lassie,—
I'll speer, if ye'll but come wi' me,
   An' ease my heart o' pain, lassie.

### VI.

My pleading's a' in vain, laddie;
   My pleading,s a' in vain, laddie;
Gae get the guid auld folk's consent,
   An' then ca' me your ain, laddie.

# A Guid New Year.

Air—" When Silent Time."

## I.

A GUID New Year to ane an' a',
　O, mony may you see,
An' during a' the years that come,
　O, happy may you be!
An' may you ne'er hae cause to mourn,
　To sigh, or shed a tear;—
To ane an' a', baith great an' sma',
　A hearty good New Year.

## II,

O, time flies fast, he winna wait,
　My friend, for you or me;
He works his wonders day by day,
　An' onward still doth flee.
O, wha can tell gin ilka ane
　I see sae happy here,
Will meet again, an' merry be,
　Anither guid New Year.

## III.

We twa hae baith been happy lang,
　We ran about the braes—
In ae wee cot, beneath a tree,
　We spent our early days;

We ran about the burnie's side,
  The spot we aye held dear;—
And those wha used to meet us there,
  We'll think on mony a year.


### VI.

Now let us hope our years may be
  As guid as they hae been;
An' let us hope we ne'er may see
  The sorrows we have seen;
An' let us hope that ane an' a'—
  Our, friends baith far and near,
May aye enjoy for time to come,
  A hearty guid New Year.


## Bonny, Bonny was the Morn.

AIR—"Blythe, blythe, and Merry was she."

### I:

BONNY, bonny was the morn
  When we rose to rin awa;
Phœbus did the hills adorn,
  Scarce a breeze o' wind did blaw.
Anna rose and slipped near me,
  "Johuny, Johnny, come," she cried,
"O, I'm fear'd the auld folk hear me;
  If they do, they'll gar us bide."

## II.

I gat ready, kiss'd my dearie,
  We each ither's fear did feel,
Bundled up our claes, and eerie,
  Bade the guid auld folk fareweel.
I had wrought and kept them canny,
  Wrought, I ween, for many a year;
For my hire I wanted Anna,
  But o' this they wadna hear.

## III.

Soon we left them—reached the balan'
  I a week before had ta'en,
God sin'syne has blest our toilin',
  We sin'syne hae baith been ane.
Soon the auld folk ceased to scorn,
  When our weel doing ways they saw;
Aye sin'syne we bless the morn,
  When we rose to rin awa.

---

# The Blooming Heather.

## I.

Bonny is the blooming heather,
  Bonny is the blooming heather;
But it's bonnier still, I ween,
  When 'mang't twa lovers meet thegither.

O, then it blooms sae fresh and fair,
 Then ilka thing around is bonny,
When the lovely lass is there
 That we lo'e mair dear than ony.

## II.

Then the bleating lambs that cry,
 Make ilk thing seem blythe and choery,
When upon the breast we lie
 O' her that we can ca' our dearie.
Bonny is the blooming heather;
 Bonny is the blooming heather,
But dearest to the youthfu' heart,
 When 'mang't twa lovers meet thegither.

---

# The Cares of Life.

## I.

Oh! why should mankind not be merry,
 As lang's he's todlin' here?
Life is at best a terrible worry;
 But yet there's nae reason to fear.

## II.

Man meets in wi' mony a hardship,
 As life's weary vale he gangs through,—
But I've aye found a gate to get out at,
 And hope that I ever will do.

## III.

It's true that we a' hae our sorrows,
  At least, for mysel' I've my share;
But the truth is, to look round about me
  There's mony a mortal has mair.

## IV.

Sad poverty presses the poor man,
  The rich winna look to their state;
But there's happiness whiles in the cottage,
  Unkend to the mighty and great.

## V.

When this life is done there's a prospect,
  A hope which all honest men have,—
A glorious land we may live in
  When laid lowly down in the grave.

~~~~~~~~~~~~~

# Oh! Winter is Come.

Air,—" Auld Rob Morris."

## I.

Oh! winter is come, an' the cauld blasts noo blaw,
  The hills o' auld Scotland are covered wi' snaw;
My ain fate resembles ilk bush and ilk tree,
  For Anna, fair Anna, ne'er smiles upon me.

L

## II.

The spring may return, an' deck a' in green,
   The hills and the vales may in beauty be seen;
But pleasure or peace they to me canna gie,
   For Anna, fair Anna, ne er smiles upon me.

## III.

O! well may my head aye be stoundin' an' sair,
   An' weel may my heart aye be beatin' wi' care,
An' weel may the tear trickle down frae my e'e,—
   For Anna, fair Anna, ne'er smiles upon me.

## IV.

But Oh! when I thin that she yet may be mine,
   When a ray of this hope in my bosom doth shine,
I ask not on earth mair pleasure to hae,
   Than Anna, fair Anna, to smile upon me.

## March of Mesmerism.

Air,—" The Spinning o't."

## I.

O, WOULD the wide warld beware o' the loons,
   Wha practice sae aften the gulling o't,
Wha come frae Auld Reekie an ither big towns,
   Their pockets—they look to the filling o't.

Those mountebank callants, wha-hastily flee
Frae city to city—frae Perth and Dundee—
And swear that ye'll something astonishing see
    If ye'll only put faith in their telling o't.

## II.

There's constantly something to tak up our time,
    Though a body has ever so little o't;
Some blundering scribblers pest us wi' ryhme,
    But o' sense they seldom show meikle o't;
The flying machine late engaged a' our care,
Which promised to bear us awa through the air;
But now the concern has blawn up, I fear,—
    High pressure has bursted the metal o't.

## III.

Mesmeric Phrenology now is the go,
    A' body's begun to the trying o't;
If the science progress in the same ratio,
    We'll no daur e'en *think* for the spying o't.
It's advocates tell us their patients can see
The folk in the moon at their toddy and tea,
Or what's to tak place in the town of Dundee,—
    There's ferlies, I wat, in the doing o't.

## IV.

If any puir wight frae his hame gangs awa'
    And offers to show them the folly o't,
The place that's no yucky he'll get it to claw,

As payment and thanks for the telling o't;
They'll stand up and swear that they'll hear him no more,
They'll howl and they'll hiss, and they'll rant and they'll
  roar,
Till the puir silly fellow is dragged to the door,—
Right glad to escape frae the melling o't.\*

## V.

I wonder, in nature, what will we hae next,—
Now folk can be "done" by the willing o't;
Teeth and legs can be drawn by the mesmeric touch,
E'en a heart may be had for the stealing o't;
For the mesmerists tell us their patients can see ·
The man o' the moon at his toddy and tea,
Or what will tak place next year in Dundee,
There's ferlies, I wat, in the doing o't.

\* About this time considerable excitement was occasioned by
the visit of itinerant lecturers on mesmerism. The poet was
then rather sceptical on the subject ; but the fact of stiff arms
and stiffer legs made him appear unsuccessful in the debates.
Nothing daunted, he resolved to try a lecture in an adjoining
town, situated on the Braes of Angus ; and for this purpose a
meeting was called, and the noveltly of the lecture drew together
a large assemblage. The lecture was begun, and a goodly
number of the Disciples of Mesmer were present. When they
saw the orator was on the negative, a noisy warfare ensued ;
which resulted in the lecturer having to beat a speedy retreat.
It may here be remarked, that a relative of the author's is preach-
ing and lecturing in the same place, with greater success on high-
er subjects, to an intelligent Christian Congregation.

# Little Children.

Little children make me glad
Though my very soul be sad;
Laughing in their sport and glee,
Climbing up upon my knee:
Running round about my chair,
With their hearts sae free frae care,
Playing wi' joy at hide and seek,
Out and in they merrily keek,
And their half-pronounced names,
Tend to cheer our humble hames.
While we soothe them wi' a sang
Winter nights are never lang;
While they prattle by our side,
Cheerful is our clean fireside;
They to bless mankind were given—
Home wi' them's a little heaven.

J. Pellow, Printer, Murraygate, Dundee.

www.ingramcontent.com/pod-product-compliance
Lightning Source LLC
Chambersburg PA
CBHW020746020726
47495CB00008B/2336